W9-AQO-102

LEADING LOYALTY

LEADING
CRACKING THE CODE TO CUSTOMER DEVOTION
LOYALTY

SANDY
ROGERS

LEENA
RINNE

SHAWN
MOON

HARPERCOLLINS
LEADERSHIP

AN IMPRINT OF HARPERCOLLINS
NEW YORK

© 2019 Franklin Covey Co.

Published by HarperCollins Leadership, an imprint of HarperCollins Focus LLC.

Book design by The Creative Lab at FranklinCovey.

ISBN 978-0-8144-3960-9 (eBook)
ISBN 978-0-8144-3939-5 (HC)

Library of Congress Cataloging-in-Publication Data

Library of Congress Control Number: 2018956213

Printed in the United States of America
19 20 21 22 23 LSC 10 9 8 7 6 5 4 3 2 1

TABLE OF CONTENTS

PART FIVE—IMPLEMENTING LOYALTY

FOREWORD

In today's hypercompetitive and connected world, where customers can switch to another provider with the click of a mouse or rethink a purchase decision based on a single online review, earning the true loyalty of customers has proven to be elusive for most organizations. In pursuit of even small gains in customer loyalty, organizations offer lower prices, provide incentives, or construct reward programs, only to find that the benefit of such measures is often muted and/or short-lived. Such measures may change customers' short-term purchase behaviors, but they rarely earn customers' real loyalty and are easily replicated by competitors.

Over the last thirty years, FranklinCovey has worked with thousands of organizations around the world to help them adopt the behaviors that can earn the genuine loyalty of their customers. FranklinCovey has also conducted research deep inside more than 1,700 organizations, conducting hundreds of matched-pair comparisons. From this front-row, real-time vantage point, we have identified three key differentiators that set loyalty-leading organizations apart from their lesser-performing counterparts. These key differentiators are:

First, loyalty leaders set the bar for what they consider a "loyal customer" much higher. Adolph Rupp, the renowned coach of the University of Kentucky men's basketball team, once observed, "Whenever you see a man on top of a mountain, you can be sure he didn't fall there." The same can be said of loyalty-leading organizations. They start by defining success not just based on satisfaction, but much more—on achieving true loyalty. Research shows that many of the organizations proudly advertising "95 percent customer satisfaction" actually have only a small percentage of customers who are truly loyal.

These organizations could more accurately state that 95 percent of their customers are *not dissatisfied*. This is an important distinction. Playing not to disappoint your customers is very different from playing to delight your customers and win their loyalty. Real loyalty is the deep, heartfelt allegiance expressed through customers who are not only satisfied, but are delighted and faithful to a company's products and services. They return time and again, expand the breadth of products or services they buy from you, refer others to you, and your relationship with them can withstand the occasional misstep or miscommunication.

Our research shows that these intensely loyal customers are the most profitable and durable portion of a successful organization's revenue. They form the strategic foundation on which any great organization is built. Loyalty-leading organizations focus on earning their customers' loyalty. This differentiates them from organizations whose focus is primarily on avoiding customer dissatisfaction.

Second, loyalty leaders recognize that the highest levels of customer loyalty are created when there is a strong human connection (whether live, remote, or digital) with their customers. We each have family members, friends, or organizations in our lives to whom we are fiercely loyal. This emotion typically comes as the natural, virtuous result of the way in which we are treated by those people or organizations. Loyalty leaders demonstrate empathy for others, take responsibility for meeting the needs of others, and act generously toward them.

Finally, loyalty leaders are much better at adopting the behaviors that most delight their customers. Our research found that every organization has pockets of great performance—divisions, regions, districts, departments, shifts, or individual leaders—that consistently create loyal customers. These pockets of great performance exist even in poorly performing companies. Conversely, no organization is perfect, and examples of variation between exceptional service and mediocre or even poor service abound. What really differentiates the loyalty leaders from their lesser-performing counterparts isn't that one organization has variability and the other doesn't; rather, it is the extent of that variability. Loyalty leaders' operations are significantly more consistent in implementing the behaviors that generate loyalty. This is because they have come to understand both the principles and practices that drive loyalty, and they authentically model them throughout their organization.

Leading Loyalty provides a blueprint for integrating these three differentiators into your organization's culture. This book will challenge you to become a true loyalty leader—with your team, in your organization, and in your personal life. It recognizes that, in order for this to occur, the principles and behaviors that generate loyalty must be practiced at the individual level.

You'll find that this book was written for two audiences. First, for everyone who interfaces with customers, both inside and outside an organization. You might work in a call center; a store or branch; or in the finance, sales, marketing, manufacturing, or IT department. Wherever you work, you have customers, and your actions impact the loyalty of your customers. And regardless of your industry—from healthcare to government, from nonprofit to the private sector—the loyalty of your customers defines your success.

Second, this book is for leaders. As a leader, your ability to craft a culture that consistently creates loyal customers begins with an understanding of the necessary behaviors and practices, and then ensures that your teams voluntarily and systematically take responsibility for implementing them with high fidelity. To this end, you'll find eleven powerful team "huddles"—quick meetings with a specific purpose—that introduce and refine the skills and tools you can use to inspire loyalty. These eleven huddles are a repeatable, proven formula for engendering the loyalty of your various customers, both personal and professional.

Through reading and applying the principles taught in this book, you will increase your ability to generate loyalty among those with whom you come in contact and, from there, create an organization that systematically creates loyalty among your customers.

AUTHORS' NOTE

Much has been written on the importance of earning and sustaining loyalty. So, why *this* book? How is *Leading Loyalty* different? To us, the distinction is clear: While the benefits of customer loyalty are generally well understood, this book will illustrate the process and tools to earn true loyalty—the kind of loyalty fueled in the heart through positive, emotional interactions with others.

In a general sense, loyalty can increase from a variety of positive customer interactions. But our research and engagements over the past twenty-five years, combined with the knowledge and expertise of our clients, colleagues, and friends, have shown that real loyalty can only be realized through the synergistic interplay of what we call the Three Core Loyalty Principles. These principles are put into practice by first adopting the Loyalty Leader Mindset and then enacting the key behaviors tied to each loyalty principle:

Loyalty Leader Mindset

- *I earn the loyalty of others by having empathy for them, taking responsibility for their needs, and being generous.*

Loyalty Principle 1: Empathy

To show empathy, we need to practice these key behaviors:

- Make a genuine human connection with people.
- Listen to learn their hidden story.

Loyalty Principle 2: Responsibility

To take responsibility, we need to practice these key behaviors:

- Discover the real job to be done (others' goals).
- Follow up to strengthen the relationship.

Loyalty Principle 3: Generosity

To be generous with other people, we need to practice these key behaviors:

- Share insights openly to help others win.

- Surprise them with unexpected extras.

Regardless of where you work, you have customers, and the loyalty of your customers defines your success. If you're a leader looking to earn loyalty more consistently throughout your organization, we invite you to draw from the various customer examples and then connect the principles and practices to your team, peers, direct reports, or other stakeholders. To facilitate this, each chapter offers tips to help leaders embrace the Three Core Loyalty Principles within their sphere of influence and responsibility.

In the pages that follow, you can expect answers to these critical questions:

- Why does loyalty really matter?

- Who is most responsible for creating loyalty?

- How can you systematically create loyalty with your employees and customers?

- How can you implement and sustain loyalty in your organization?

Whether you manage other people or not, you can embrace the Loyalty Leader Mindset and find that customers and coworkers will not only like you, but *love* you as a result. We use this word *love* intentionally to indicate their intense feeling of loyalty. This gets to the heart of what it means to have others who are loyal to you. It is our sincere desire that, as you put this book into practice, you'll come to experience the joy of having others who are *truly* loyal to you.

PART
ONE

THE FOUNDATION FOR LEADING LOYALTY

INTRODUCTION

REAL LOYALTY IS POWERED BY PEOPLE

In a suburb of a metropolitan city, two big warehouse stores sit next to each other on the same side of a main thoroughfare. They both sell the same stuff: groceries, clothes, books, electronics, drugs, toys, even furniture. The stores are about the same size, the parking areas identical—same location, same footprint, same sorts of products—yet one store flourishes while the other struggles to stay alive. What's going on here?

When asked why their store is virtually deserted, the managers of Store 2 have all kinds of answers. "It's Amazon. It's online retailers. They're driving brick-and-mortar stores like ours out of business. Malls are closing everywhere; you can't find good workers; millennials have no work ethic. The higher-ups rely on discounts too much. They don't advertise enough. . . ."

Yet, right next door, Store 1 is buzzing and booming with business. What's the difference? Let's walk inside the two stores and see for ourselves.

Store 2 is quiet. A single cashier lounges against her counter, wearing earphones and looking bored. A couple of customers are picking through things, squinting at tiny labels. You notice one customer who wants to return a purchase walking up to a big desk with a sign that reads "Customer Service." She stands there for a while, shifting her weight, looking around, wondering if anyone will notice her. She clears her throat loudly. Eventually, the woman calls out, "Is anyone here?"

A tired-looking man slouches out of a back room. "Can I help you?" he asks in a voice so despondent he could be in mourning.

Now let's pay a visit to Store 1. Eager, intent customers are pouring inside. A greeter smiles at people as they enter and occasionally stops to answer a question or give directions. Inside, it looks like a warehouse, but large-print signs show the prices of everything. There's a big difference in the employees. All are wearing blue vests, and they move with a spring in their step, smiling as they go. These energetic employees are running errands for customers, directing customers, and even joking with them. We notice a man hesitating over the flower bouquets on sale, and a blue-vested guy stops and says: "I just brought in some fresh new ones. They're right back here." He leads the delighted customer to the next aisle.

Elsewhere, more mature women and men are pleasantly handing out free samples of smoked ham or Spanish cheese or tater tots with truffle oil as people crowd around them. At the customer service desk, a customer is apologetically returning a purchase. The bright, perky person behind the desk takes it, asks no questions, doesn't require a receipt, and thanks her for bringing it back, with a genuine wish for a good day.

Store 1 is a Costco store—a company that *Barron's* reports has "generated fierce loyalty among both shoppers and staff while rewarding long-term investors."[1] In retail, the chance of keeping an employee for more than a year is about 45 percent. At Costco, however, it's 94 percent. And 91 percent of Costco customers renew their membership every year, making Costco "the world's customer-retention record holder."[2]

A client of ours mentioned that he and his wife go to Costco every Saturday.

"Why?" we asked.

"Because that's where I see all my friends." It has become a gathering place for him and his neighbors. That is a picture of real loyalty.

How does Costco, in an industry with notoriously unhappy workers, keep its employees so loyal and happy? How has it created a loyalty culture that seems to permeate nearly every employee and customer interaction? The answer is simple: Costco enjoys loyalty because it has embraced the Loyalty Leader Mindset and put the Three Core Loyalty Principles into practice.

For example, Costco took a clear stand on how it would treat its employees with empathy, responsibility, and generosity when it decided to pay more than twice the salary of average retailers and provide benefits, too. When Wall Street worried that Costco's "over-generous" treatment of employees might cut into shareholder returns, founder Jim Sinegal replied, "We want to . . . take care of our customers, take care of our people, and respect our suppliers. And we think if we do those things pretty much in that order, that we're going to reward shareholders."[3] And they did. If you had invested $1,000 in Costco when it went public in 1985, that investment would be worth around $100,000 by 2018.

How was Costco able to grow 40 percent per year during the same years that online shopping exploded? Why is Costco, which is subject to all the same pressures Store 2 is struggling with, thriving? Costco has intentionally built a comprehensive system that engenders loyalty among its employees and customers. Similar things could be said about many other loyalty winners in hundreds of organizations— retailers, restaurants, realtors, car-rental companies, business service providers, schools, hospitals—whose customers and employees would have emotional breakdowns if the organization closed its doors. The Three Core Loyalty Principles for earning loyalty are the same every-where. We see them at work in every organization that earns the most committed customers, and the most engaged employees.

Author and researcher Seth Godin makes a useful distinction between two kinds of loyalty. The first kind of loyalty is the loyalty of convenience. "I'm going to look around, sure, but probably won't switch. Switching is risky; it's time-consuming. Switching means I might make a mistake or lose my [frequent flyer] miles or have to defend a new decision." Convenience loyalty results simply from habit: We can take the same bus every day and still hate the bus company. One executive with whom we work likes to say, "Inertia is not loyalty!"

Godin describes the second kind of loyalty—what we recognize as true loyalty—as, "I'm not looking, and I'm not even inter-ested in looking." This is the loyalty of someone who doesn't want to know there's a better deal somewhere else. This type of loyalty is more anchored in emotional commitment than inertia. Doesn't that describe how we feel about our favorite brand or business? Discounts and reward programs are easy to offer, and while they may bring repeat business, they alone will not create the kind of emotionally intense allegiance that is a hallmark of real loyalty.

Suppose you are dining in a restaurant and find a hair in your soup. Depending on your loyalty to that restaurant, you would likely react differently, wouldn't you?

If you'd never been there before, or you just go there out of con-venience, you might complain and ask for a new bowl of soup. Or just get up and walk out.

If you've had an unpleasant history with that restaurant, you might react with anger. "This is disgusting! I will never eat here again, and others are going to hear about this." You might take a picture of the hairy soup, post it on social media, and do your best to make sure everyone you know sees it.

But suppose you're a regular at this restaurant. They know what you like, often going out of their way to please you in unexpected ways. You've told many others what a great place this is. You bring your family and friends here. They've never let you down before. Now you find a hair in the soup. How do you react? You might point it out kindly and quietly to the server, who apologizes profusely and brings you a new bowl of soup. You might tell yourself it's a once-in-a-million mistake and shrug it off. You might just ignore and forgive it; you love this place and, after all, everyone makes mistakes occasionally.

So, what drives your reaction in each of these situations? In the first case, it's indifference; in the second case, suspicion and disgust. But in the third case, it's loyalty.

Emotionally intense feelings often come through our interactions with people. We feel it when we engage with them. They welcome us, smile at us, and speak kindly and respectfully to us. They go out of their way to greet us and make things easy for us. They are so nice, so accommodating, that we start to wonder, *Who are these people? Where do they find people like this?*

Why do we love them? Often because *they love us*!

We also feel it when they *don't* love us—when they're indifferent; when at best they give us a tight smile and a "Have a good day," or when at worst they ignore us, mess up our order, quote policy to us, or find some excuse not to serve us. Most annoying are times when people refuse to take responsibility for our poor experience.

When American Express studied 1,620 customers under laboratory conditions, 63 percent said "they felt their heart rate increase when they thought about receiving great customer service." These thoughts "triggered the same cerebral reactions as feeling *loved*. The takeaway? When it comes to customer service, it's not about what customers think. Great service is about *feelings*."[4]

As customers, we are so love-starved that we are simply amazed, even shocked, when we encounter a genuine, caring voice on the helpline or a kind face across the service desk. The pulse quickens. We're flooded with warmth. We are so accustomed to apathetic faces and impersonal, formula-spouting voices that we can be truly overwhelmed by the opposite.

In a study commissioned by Oracle, when asked what makes a memorable experience that causes consumers to stick with a brand, 73 percent of the people interviewed said, "Friendly employees or customer-service representatives." When reflecting on our own personal customer-service experiences—when we've been exceptionally happy or overwhelmingly frustrated—we tend to think about the people involved in the interaction. Of course, the products and services, policies and procedures, computer systems, billing, and price structure can anger or delight us, too, but it is most often the people who shape how we feel about an organization. This book focuses on the intense positive emotion that can be created through our personal engagement with other people.

Is your behavior earning your customers' loyalty? How about the behavior of the people on your team?

Fred Reichheld, Bain Fellow and founder of Bain & Company's Loyalty practice, has made a strong case for loyalty and its powerful impact on growth and bottom-line results. Our contribution to this topic comes by examining *the specific underlying principles that drive loyalty*, enabling the reader to crack the code to customer devotion. These principles are both timeless and universal.

Throughout this book, we'll outline how the Loyalty Leader Mindset (Part One) is expressed through the synergistic interplay of the Three Core Loyalty Principles (Parts Two, Three, and Four). This interaction provides the spark to ignite loyalty between you, your coworkers, and customers. But to fully appreciate the Three Core Loyalty Principles, you must adopt the mindset that allows them to flourish in the first place.

CHAPTER 1

LOYALTY LEADER MINDSET

"IT'S NOT ENOUGH FOR YOUR CUSTOMERS
TO LIKE YOU—THEY HAVE TO LOVE YOU."
—CATHERINE NELSON, EXECUTIVE LEADERSHIP CONSULTANT

The paradigm we choose greatly influences how we see and react to the world around us. The Loyalty Leader Mindset can be expressed as:

> I earn the loyalty of others by having empathy for them, taking responsibility for their needs, and being generous.

Our mindset relative to loyalty is profoundly influenced by our understanding of the answers to these questions:

- Do you believe loyalty is essential to your success?
- Who do you feel is most responsible for creating loyalty?
- How can you earn loyalty from your customers and colleagues?

WHY DOES LOYALTY MATTER?

Our team at FranklinCovey joined with the Coca-Cola Retailing Research Councils to do a major study[1] asking this question: Why do seemingly similar retail stores produce such different results?

We collected data from a cross-section of more than 300,000 employees in 5,000 work teams from 1,100 chain stores. We took the competitive environment of each store into account. We combined this data with customer- and employee-loyalty data and financial data, looking to identify the "great performers" among these stores.

What did we find? We found great performers, all right. Just not very many of them. It was like looking out over a campground at night. It's pitch dark, but here and there a campfire dots the landscape. Our findings were like that. We did see bright patches—stores that stood out from the rest in terms of revenues, profitability, and customer and employee loyalty—but they were few and far between. We called these "campfire" stores. Something was burning there that we didn't find in the average stores.

And we found something else: *The customers of those campfire stores were incredibly loyal.*

Stores with high customer-loyalty scores—both in general and especially relative to their toughest competitors—are rewarded handsomely. In fact, if the average stores in a chain could raise their loyalty scores just a quarter of the way toward those of the campfire stores, overall profitability would rise a stunning 20 to 30 percent!

So, do campfire stores just happen? Does lightning unexpectedly hit in those stores? No, of course not. We found that the top-performing campfire stores earn a lot more loyalty because they deliberately focus on earning loyalty—not by chance, but by choice. We'll explain how they do that throughout the rest of this book. But you can be sure they start with clarity about exactly what a great customer experience looks and feels like.

Because here's the irony: In a Bain survey of 362 top executives, 85 percent believed their companies delivered "a superior customer experience." The really astonishing part? Only 8 percent of their customers agreed with them.[2]

Are corporate executives really that out of touch? Maybe, but perhaps they don't define "superior customer experience" the way their customers do. The execs are probably looking at satisfaction metrics, which are more about "lack of dissatisfaction" than about experiences that earn true loyalty.

Of course, all good managers work to satisfy customers, and many do this pretty well. But at the same time, they frequently make a bad assumption—they figure that if customers aren't dissatisfied, they must be getting a "superior experience"; they must be happy, loyal fans. But just because your kid doesn't get Ds and Fs doesn't mean he or she is a great student. Likewise, there's a big difference between not disappointing customers and earning their loyalty.

For example, one hotel company was always saying they got "94 percent guest satisfaction," but when they started to measure true loyalty, they found that 94 percent guest satisfaction really meant "94 percent non-dissatisfaction." Only 18 percent of their customers were truly loyal. This hotel chain was claiming victory on the customer-service front, while a few competitor hotels that were deliberately focused on creating real loyalty were eating their lunch.

Even your regular customers are not necessarily loyal. The relationship between regular customers and profitability is weaker than most of us believe, according to a four-year Harvard research study involving 16,000 people: "About half of those customers who made regular purchases for at least two years—and were therefore designated as 'loyal'—barely generated a profit."[3]

However, customers with the *attitude* of loyalty are incredibly profitable. "Customers who scored high on both actual and attitudinal measures of loyalty generated 120 percent more profit than those whose loyalty was observed through transactions alone."[4] This is not just a business-to-consumer phenomena; it's true in the business-to-business world as well.

Patrons with deep loyalty glow when they talk about you. And they are not just your customers—they're advocates, believers, activists, campaigners, sponsors, friends, and fans. One of our associates told us, "When Costco announced they were opening a store in my town, I literally cried with joy." *That* is the attitude we're talking about. When these people go out to dinner with friends and loved ones, they excitedly tell stories about their experiences with organizations they love.

As Bain & Company's Fred Reichheld wrote, "Loyal customers come back more often, buy more products, refer their friends, provide valuable feedback, cost less to serve, and are less price-sensitive." Think of the impact to your work and your organization if more of your customers behaved in these ways. But just how much does loyalty matter to the bottom line? Reichheld calls truly loyal customers "promoters"—they not only purchase a lot from you, but they enthusiastically send other customers your way, too. By contrast, he calls habitual customers "passives" and your least loyal customers "detractors." In his detailed research, Reichheld found that promoters are about four times more profitable to your bottom line. So if we're discussing your profits, then, yes, loyalty really matters. And earning loyalty starts by adopting the Loyalty Leader Mindset and living the Three Core Loyalty Principles.

WHO IS MOST RESPONSIBLE FOR CREATING LOYALTY?

The CEO, right? Well, certainly he or she plays an important role. Don Ross, vice chairman of the company that owns the Enterprise, National, and Alamo car-rental brands, says the "CEO should set the example, create the environment for loyalty, and extend trust to all leaders of customer-facing staff." A commitment to promoting people whose love for customers is contagious has certainly served Enterprise Rent-A-Car well. And love for customers is expressed not only through personal interactions, but also through the creation of policies, processes, and technology that make it easy for customers to do business with the organization. The CEO plants the fertile field that nourishes these activities and outcomes for customers.

But the CEO is not the primary driver of the loyalty we are talking about in this book. It's all of us—the people who serve customers inside and outside the organization every day. A major study by the Corporate Executive Board concludes that "the brilliant battle plans created by the generals at company headquarters will either succeed or fail based on the actions of hundreds or even thousands of foot soldiers."[5]

Bain and Gallup have found that, in most organizations, the further you move down the hierarchy from the CEO to the front line, the lower the employee engagement and loyalty to the organization. And people who are customer-facing—the very ones who have the biggest impact on the customer experience—*are usually the lowest-paid, least-trained, and least-engaged employees.*

Turnover among these employees is more than 150 percent per year in some organizations. Needless to say, with one foot out the door, a frontline employee may not be riveted on building long-term customer relationships. As our friend Shep Hyken frequently says, "The customer experience rarely exceeds the employee experience."

Over the years, Fred Reichheld's work has shown that companies with a lot of "promoter" customers have their "promoter" employees to thank for it.[6] Like promoter customers, promoter employees love you, talk you up, and recommend you to their friends. They stay with you and serve your customers with zeal and energy. They are by far the most important factor in gaining customer loyalty. Many experts recommend that "one focus of your company's marketing strategy should be developing brand ambassadors and making sure they are involved in social conversations. . . . Most of the time when you think of a brand ambassador, you probably think of someone with huge influence or name recognition, like a celebrity, who is paid for their efforts to promote a brand. While influencer marketing like this is still popular, brand ambassadors can also be customers and, just as importantly, employees."[7] While there are many complex variables that produce your bottom-line profits, there's no question that your customer-facing employees play a critically important role.

In our work at FranklinCovey, we found that truly loyal customers are rarely found in places without strongly committed employees, and the behavior of employees directly serving customers is often the deciding factor in whether customers are loyal. Again and again, customers of the great-performing chain locations we studied talked about helpful and friendly employees. They also mentioned things that were the result of frontline employees who care—cleanliness, no waiting, items on the shelf.

There's a difference, however, between being "happy" with your job and having a Loyalty Leader Mindset. We asked the employees in thousands of stores about their job satisfaction, and correlated the results with their store customer-loyalty scores. To our surprise, we initially found little connection. In fact, some of the stores where the employees were happiest were actually floundering when it came to customer loyalty.

Then our partner Dick Rennecamp suggested we add a question to the next employee survey to learn whether the employees in each store *knew* their customer-loyalty score. Dick's hypothesis was that if employees don't know their customer-loyalty score, they're probably not very engaged in improving it. As anyone can observe on a basketball court in a city park, people play harder when they're keeping score.

Dick's theory proved correct. In the 41 percent of the 3,500 stores where the team members knew their customer-loyalty score, there was a direct correlation between the store's employee-loyalty score and their customer-loyalty score. But in the 59 percent of stores where the team did not know the customer-loyalty score, there was no relationship. We learned that employees must not only love their job, but be engaged in making customers happy, too. Employees may love their job because they like the benefits and can chitchat with friends all day, but that doesn't bode well for the customer experience.

So, whose job is it to inspire employees to do a great job for customers? You may say, "The manager, of course." No question, the team leader is the linchpin—the leverage point—in building team culture and inspiring everyone to do their best for customers. But what if you don't have an inspiring team leader? Can you make a real difference in your team's ability to earn customer loyalty? The answer is most definitely *yes*. And not just in your own engagement with customers, but also, and perhaps even more important, in your interactions with your fellow team members.

"Leadership is a choice, not a position," the cofounder of our company, Stephen R. Covey, was fond of saying. The company can give you a title, but that doesn't make you a leader. As one of our clients once said: "You are not the leader you think you are. You're the leader your people think you are."

Anyone can adopt a Loyalty Leader Mindset. You don't need a formal title. You can be the most experienced executive in the company or the cashier who was just hired yesterday. It doesn't matter. A loyalty leader earns loyalty from others by living the principles that acknowledge their worth and limitless potential. An assistant to an assistant hairdresser in a barbershop can be true to the Loyalty Leader Mindset if he is trustworthy, responsible, and generous in dealing with customers. Likewise, the CEO can be a loyalty leader if she practices empathy and takes ownership of customers' issues. After his son Bill became CEO of Marriott, J. Willard Marriott, the founder and chairman, spent his time personally responding to customers who had a disappointing experience at a Marriott Hotel. He was a loyalty leader.

But in all cases, leaders have to *choose* to adopt this mindset. In fact, too many formally designated leaders operate through an ineffective or even harmful paradigm. You may have heard that "people don't quit companies; they quit their manager." The research bears this out. According to Gallup, "Managers account for at least 70 percent of variance in employee-engagement scores across business units. This variation is in turn responsible for severely low worldwide employee engagement."[8]

If you are a manager, how are you doing as a loyalty leader? Using a 0 to 10 scale (10 indicates "extremely likely"), how likely would your employees be to recommend you? Using the same scale, how likely would your customers be to recommend you? Would more than 60 percent give you a score of 9 or 10? More than 80 percent?

Ultimately, your financial results and your performance reviews will depend on the answer to this question: Are you a leader who earns loyalty from your employees and customers?

To change the behavior, engagement, and loyalty of employees, the leader's mindset and resulting behaviors need to change. Many managers get their jobs because they're technically skilled, but they may not have learned how to model, teach, and reinforce the behaviors needed to earn the loyalty of others. Employee loyalty comes from genuinely caring about their thoughts and ideas, sincerely wanting to understand their goals, then helping employees achieve them. It comes from a willingness to appreciate employees' contributions.

Just as true loyalty comes from feelings deep inside you, the power to inspire loyalty comes from deep inside as well. *It's fundamentally a question of the kind of person you choose to be.*

You'll find that winning the heart of every customer and colleague begins with you. At FranklinCovey, we teach that "as long as you think the problem is out there, that very thought is the problem." Too often we blame the team or the strategic hand we're dealt or the higher-ups or the weather for problems that actually have their origins in *ourselves*. Remember the store with the empty parking lot next to Costco? That is exactly what those store employees were telling themselves: The problem was out there, *not in here.*

The damaging paradigm that earning loyalty requires others to change is self-defeating. But once you shift to a mindset that loyalty requires *you* to change *first*—well, it's liberating. It's in your control. You have the exciting challenge of becoming a person who inspires loyalty. You have it in your power to build a team of loyal employees, no matter what kind of leaders you have or what kind of fate the company's recruiters have dealt you.

You might already be that 1-in-10 leader who naturally inspires the loyalty of other people, but most of us are not. It doesn't mean we're bad people—it just means we haven't necessarily focused on the principles that drive loyalty. We might be very talented operationally. We might be strategic, organized, disciplined, and highly productive. But unless we live by the principles that kindle loyalty in the hearts of others, we are unlikely to enrich the lives of our customers and employees, or our own life for that matter.

Here are ten questions to help you gauge how effective you are at earning the loyalty of other people:

LOYALTY SELF-CHECK

Rate yourself on a scale of **1** to **5**. A **5** means "That's me exactly."
A **1** means "That's not me at all." Nobody will ever see your
answers, so be honest with yourself.

1. I'm very sensitive to what other people feel.	1 2 3 4 5
2. I connect quickly and easily with other people.	1 2 3 4 5
3. I'm a good listener, very interested in what other people have to say.	1 2 3 4 5
4. I take my responsibilities very seriously and do my best to carry them out.	1 2 3 4 5
5. I work at solving problems without avoiding them or giving up.	1 2 3 4 5
6. I work hard at building relationships with customers and coworkers.	1 2 3 4 5
7. I am generous with others, freely giving my time and talents to help them.	1 2 3 4 5
8. I openly share my thoughts and ideas in the spirit of being helpful.	1 2 3 4 5
9. I often do something a little extra for people to show them I care.	1 2 3 4 5
10. I would recommend anyone to do business with my team.	1 2 3 4 5
TOTAL	

🔍 LOYALTY SELF-CHECK KEY

When you finish, add your scores and see how you did on the scoring key below.

40–50	You are doing a good job of creating loyalty, but you could always do better.
30–39	You probably have an uneven record of creating loyalty in others.
20–29	You have a lot of people who don't care one way or the other about doing business with you.
10–19	You are probably losing customers and employees at an unhealthy rate.

HOW CAN YOU EARN THE LOYALTY OF YOUR COLLEAGUES AND CUSTOMERS?

Principles rule the world. Gravity is a principle that works on us whether we like it or not. Even if we choose not to believe in it and jump off a building, we'll still fall. In the same way, principles apply to everybody, regardless of our background, our life experience, or our beliefs. Principles also rule our relationships with people. If we ignore or violate those principles, we will fail. The Three Core Loyalty Principles for earning loyalty in any relationship are:

- Empathy
- Responsibility
- Generosity

True loyalty is the natural consequence of principled behavior. Principled behavior awakens loyalty much more effectively than reward points or promotions. Through our research, we've found that customers and employees are loyal to organizations and people who show empathy for them, take responsibility for their work, and act generously. These are not just techniques—they are behaviors that can be learned and adopted by anyone in your organization. In the chapters that follow, we'll drill down into each of the Three Core Loyalty Principles and the practices that go with each one. Here's a preview:

LOYALTY PRINCIPLE 1: EMPATHY

We earn the loyalty of our customers and coworkers when we have empathy for them—the power not only to hear what they are saying, but also to feel what they feel. We shift our thinking from apathy to empathy. To show empathy, we need to do these two things:

Make a Genuine Human Connection. We earn loyalty when we connect with people in a warm, human, positive way. *Authentic* connections can transform a group of disengaged workers into a truly customer-centric team.

Listen to Learn the Hidden Story. Listening to understand is the key to empathy. We earn loyalty from our customers and colleagues when listening to truly learn each other's needs, concerns, and stories. We treat people differently when we know their stories, often hidden from view until others feel comfortable enough to share them with us.

LOYALTY PRINCIPLE 2: RESPONSIBILITY

We earn loyalty when we take ownership for what should be done. We don't simply give people what they ask for; instead, we *own* the goals and outcome for our customers and colleagues. We actively teach others how to take responsibility themselves. To take responsibility, we need to do these two things:

Discover the Real Job to Be Done. What people ask for may not be what they really need. A customer in a hardware store asks to buy a wrench. Unless we find out what job they want the wrench to do, we don't know which wrench they need or if they need a wrench at all. To serve a customer or coworker responsibly, we need to ask thoughtful questions so we know what job they need us to do for them.

Follow Up to Strengthen the Relationship. We make the relationship stronger by following up. It shows we care about the customer's or coworker's experience and want to learn from it to improve. Uncovering problems is an especially opportune time to demonstrate our commitment to making things right and exceeding expectations.

LOYALTY PRINCIPLE 3: GENEROSITY

We earn loyalty when we are generous with others. By giving from our heart and giving more than is necessary or expected, we transform customers and coworkers into *advocates*. We delight in finding ways to make other people's lives easier and better. To be generous with other people, we need to do these two things:

Share Insights Openly. We share ideas and information that help others learn and improve. When motivated by a spirit of genuine generosity, feedback is seen as a gift. Sharing our knowledge to help customers fix a problem can engender intense feelings of loyalty.

Surprise with Unexpected Extras. We constantly experiment with new and creative ways to show people we care about them. We give "extras" that cost little—sending personal messages, remembering names, testing new surprises. Simple things like these can endear us to our customers and associates.

If you're wondering whether empathy, responsibility, and generosity are really fundamental principles of loyalty, imagine doing the opposite. Imagine treating everyone *apathetically, irresponsibly,* and *selfishly.* It's been done—in fact, it's done all the time—but it's not going to earn us loyalty. In fact, it drives customers and employees away. If we intentionally focus on living by these loyalty principles, we will earn loyalty as a matter of course. Loyal customers and colleagues will naturally gravitate to us.

WHAT HAPPENS WHEN WE ADOPT A LOYALTY LEADER MINDSET

Whether we have a formal leadership role or not, we become a loyalty leader when we adopt the Loyalty Leader Mindset and then model, teach, and reinforce the Three Core Loyalty Principles. If we're in a customer-facing role, by doing a few simple things that turn ten customers a day toward real loyalty, in a week we've created seventy new promoters! And if we manage ten employees who, by doing a few simple things, turn ten customers a day toward true loyalty, every day we create a hundred new advocates! Creating new advocates every day establishes the foundation for becoming a loyalty leader.

We've worked with thousands of organizations globally, and here's what we know: Creating customer and employee loyalty is an absolutely essential component to long-term success. Maybe it would surprise you to know that working hard to earn the loyalty of others can actually make you a happier and more fulfilled person, too. We challenge you to commit to live the principles of empathy, responsibility, and generosity in your own life, and to bring your team along for the ride. It doesn't matter who you are—a CEO, a division manager, a team leader, or *anyone* who is customer-facing—you serve the needs of other people, and you need their loyalty. It doesn't matter where you go or whom you serve—imagine what would happen if you practiced these principles at home. The principles of loyalty are the same.

MODEL, TEACH, REINFORCE, AND HIRE FOR LOYALTY

How do you instill these principles into a team? Earning loyalty is much more than teaching lessons in good service techniques. It's far more than giving everyone a copy of *Customer Service for Dummies* and ordering the team to smile and say, "Have a nice day." Your challenge is to model, teach, reinforce, and hire for the loyalty principles.

Modeling. You might be saying to yourself, "I am already empathic. I am responsible, and I am generous." Or you may feel committed to developing these behaviors in yourself. As a result, you can be a model for the members of your team, and they benefit from that more than anything. Of course, none of us is as good at living by these principles as we could be, and few of us consciously focus on them deliberately, making them the foundation of our lives. So your first challenge is to do that—to become even more the empathic, responsible, generous person you can be. Most of us have a ways to go. But that shouldn't discourage us. We can be more deeply good. We can listen better. We can make others feel more valued. And as we do so, we become the example, the *model* of what it takes to earn the loyalty of others.

Teaching. Most of us work as part of a team, so the second challenge is to build a team around us that also lives by these principles. If you are an individual team member, you can live by these principles and teach others by example. "I'm not a teacher," you say? Yes, you are. You can't help being a teacher: Your example influences the behavior of other people all day long. If you are a manager, you are, in fact, a teacher, whether you like it or not. Besides, there are real upsides to becoming a good teacher. For one thing, you're the manager: The members of your team are going to pay attention when you teach because they know if *you* value these principles, they need to do the same. The biggest upside: When you teach a principle, *you* own it, *you* internalize it, *you* learn the most. The principle becomes part of you.

Reinforcing. The third challenge is to reinforce the loyalty principles—all the time. When you praise a team member for showing responsibility, that's reinforcement. When you notice team members being less than empathic, you take them aside and gently remind them of the principle. When you see a generous act, you celebrate it with the team and say, "Now that's what we want to see!" Here are reinforcement tips you can apply to every lesson in this book:

- Hold loyalty huddles (which we describe in the next section) regularly and often.

- Recognize team members who share and contribute to building loyalty. Try to catch them in the act and celebrate it. You'll encourage others to do the same and create a culture where loyalty behaviors are celebrated continuously.

- Point to your customer- and employee-loyalty measures. Are they improving as your team members share insights and act on them? As you celebrate team members' success in living the loyalty principles?

- Coach individuals in private on ideas for building loyalty with customers and coworkers.

Hiring. If you are in a position to hire, the loyalty principles ought to be your main criteria for bringing people onto the team. For example, Progressive Insurance changed its claims-adjustor hiring profile from "cop/investigator" to "nurse." Business researcher and author Jim Collins says the most important thing to look for in a new hire is "alignment with your core ideology and values."[9] In your case, this means hiring people who are empathic, responsible, and generous. You start out way ahead if they already live by these principles. When interviewing candidates, ask for examples from past experience where their actions exhibited each principle. For example, "Please tell me about a time when you showed empathy to a customer and the impact it had. Please tell me about when you took personal responsibility for a customer issue, and it earned that customer's loyalty."

Even if you have no control over hiring, remember that you still have control over the most important ingredient to earning loyalty: your own behavior and the example you set for your team.

THE LOYALTY HUDDLE

You can bring the Loyalty Leader Mindset into practice by holding short, targeted meetings—huddles, if you will—to teach and reteach the loyalty principles to your team. "More meetings," you ask? Exactly. A brief weekly, or even daily, huddle to move the needle on customer loyalty is the key to influencing loyalty behavior.

One bank in Latin America was watching one in five customers walk away from them. Profits were sagging. Over a two-year period, the bank focused on building customer loyalty; its profitability improved by double digits, and customer churn dropped by 20 percent. How did the bank do it? By improving their customer experience based on ideas generated from customer-facing employees.

Currently, hundreds of teams within the bank's offices and branches hold daily huddles. In these fifteen-minute discussions, they talk through results and key performance indicators, many of which relate to customer experience. They also bring to the surface improvement ideas and share customer-experience stories that reinforce the customer-service culture.[10] Clearly, consistent daily emphasis on building loyalty is making a big difference for this bank.

Loyalty huddles are catching on among our clients and in many other organizations.

We recommend you lead *eleven targeted huddles* with your team, each designed to strengthen a skill from the first eleven chapters in this book:

Chapter 1 Huddle—Loyalty Leader Mindset

Chapter 2 Huddle—The Need for Empathy

Chapter 3 Huddle—Make a Genuine Human Connection

Chapter 4 Huddle—Listen to Learn the Hidden Story

Chapter 5 Huddle—The Need for Responsibility

Chapter 6 Huddle—Discover the Real Job to Be Done

Chapter 7 Huddle—Follow Up to Strengthen the Relationship

Chapter 8 Huddle—The Need for Generosity

Chapter 9 Huddle—Share Insights Openly

Chapter 10 Huddle—Surprise with Unexpected Extras

Chapter 11 Huddle—Your Legacy as a Loyalty Leader

WHAT SHOULD YOU DO IN THESE LOYALTY HUDDLES? THE AGENDA IS BRIEF BUT CONSISTENT

1. Celebrate.
2. Learn.
3. Commit.
4. Schedule follow-up.

CELEBRATE

First, recognize success in increasing loyalty and applying the principle or practice discussed in the most recent huddle. Most important, celebrate individuals who are creating customer promoters.

Why celebrate? Because study after study shows that employees are more engaged by recognition of their efforts than by anything else—including money. In one major survey, salary actually ranked eighth on the list![11] Gallup recommends that no one should go without recognition for more than seven days, and that it should come from every direction and be delivered in the way the person likes to receive appreciation. Such recognition should be "timely, to ensure that the employee knows the significance of the recent achievement."[12] Be generous about celebrating successes, and you will see more of them. Customer service expert Micah Solomon advised:

> It's not always what's measured that improves; it's what's *celebrated.* The greatest organizations have become great in part by building into their schedules opportunities to celebrate employees when they go the extra mile for customers.[13]

LEARN

The next agenda item in the loyalty huddle is to learn about a principle or practice that creates loyalty. Assign a team member to read a chapter in this book ahead of time and then lead the huddle. Everyone knows that the teacher learns more than the student, so if everyone takes a turn leading the huddle, you can be confident that they are internalizing the loyalty principles. As the great management thinker Peter Drucker observed:

> **Service people learn the most when they teach. The best way to improve the productivity of the star salesperson is for him or her to present "the secrets of my success" at a sales convention. The best way for the surgeon to improve his or her performance is to give a talk about it at the medical society. The best way for a nurse to improve her performance is to teach her fellow nurses.[14]**

In the huddle, invite team members to share any insights they may have from observing or following up with customers. "What are we learning? What is working well for customers? What should we improve?" As team members celebrate their victories, be sure to offer insights that will help the whole team improve performance.

COMMIT

The third item on the huddle agenda is to make commitments to apply what was learned in the huddle to create more customer promoters. "What could each of us commit to do this week? What new things should we try?" Note how important it is to follow through on commitments made in the huddles. Let your team members know that you expect them to keep their commitments and that they will be reporting on them in the huddles. Of course, you are the model of commitment keeping; if you fail to keep your promises, team members will automatically have permission to do the same.

SCHEDULE FOLLOW-UP

Before leaving the huddle, make sure you schedule the next huddle meeting and assign a person to read the chapter ahead of time to lead that huddle.

Once you complete all eleven huddles, repeat the process so that everyone on your team gets a chance to lead each one. We recognize that you may have very little time to teach your team about the Three Core Loyalty Principles, but carving out just ten minutes for each huddle weaves these crucial principles and practices into the fabric of your team culture. We have provided a "huddle agenda" in each chapter to help you with this process.

The managers at one of our valued resort clients hold weekly loyalty huddles with their supervisors, who then run the huddles with customer-facing teams. Here is their reaction to the huddle process:

> **Management loves it because they can choose certain topics that need special attention. The employees have created a display board where they can post comments on ways they are "listening to learn" and "making a human connection." The huddle is just a simple conversation, only ten minutes a week. You can see the enthusiasm in the employees.**[15]

How important are these huddles? Picture a team determined to increase customer loyalty. They huddle once a week and celebrate team members who are creating promoters. If the team has a customer-loyalty number, they track it to see if their new behaviors are making a difference. They talk about any service failures and what was learned. They come up with new ideas and commit to try them. New employees join the team, momentum builds, and the huddle discussions become richer and more meaningful each week.

Kick off each huddle by sharing things that stood out to you from the chapter. What was interesting? What was surprising? Then use the outline and questions below to guide your team discussion. Don't worry that you don't have all the answers. Just ask the questions and point out that you and your team are on this learning journey together. Most of all, have fun in the huddle so the team looks forward to the next one. After completing all eleven huddles the first time, discussions will become even more interesting and interactive the second time around as team members see the Three Core Loyalty Principles and practices coming to life in their interactions with customers and, perhaps even more important, with one another.

It's time to begin. Here is the agenda for your first team huddle:

HUDDLE 1—LOYALTY LEADER MINDSET

I earn true loyalty by having empathy for others, taking responsibility for their needs, and being generous.

1. **CELEBRATE**

   Celebrate people doing a great job of earning customer loyalty.

2. **LEARN**

   Discuss the following questions:

   a. What makes a customer loyal? How important is our behavior?

   b. How do promoter, passive, and detractor customers behave?

   c. Does our team have loyalty measures? If so, what are they telling us?

   d. What are we learning from our interactions with customers?

3. **COMMIT**

   Create a customer promoter.

4. **SCHEDULE FOLLOW-UP**

   Huddle 2 date/time? Who will lead?

PART
TWO

THE PRINCIPLE OF EMPATHY

CHAPTER 2

THE NEED FOR EMPATHY

"YOU CAN ONLY UNDERSTAND PEOPLE
IF YOU FEEL THEM IN YOURSELF."
—JOHN STEINBECK

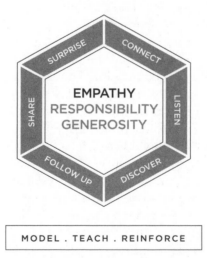

MODEL . TEACH . REINFORCE

It's feelings that drive most purchases. Perhaps we'd like to think we are all rational and entirely logical beings—that we make sound buying decisions based on facts and analysis. In reality, it's just not so. Behavioral economics shows us that, in many cases, we are anything but rational, and that our emotions are a critical part of decision making. Neurologists have identified that the decision to buy is made in the limbic part of the brain—the primitive, more emotional area that doesn't respond well to analysis or rational thought. Interestingly, if the limbic system is damaged, a person struggles with two things—emotions and decisions—which shows how intertwined these things are.

But the decision-making center of the brain does respond to empathy, the first of the Three Core Loyalty Principles. Empathy is our ability to understand and share the feelings of another person. We may not agree with the person, but we get where they're coming from. More than that, we feel what the other person feels. For the other person, it's almost like they're looking in a mirror: We reflect their feelings as if we felt similarly ourselves. Habit 5 of FranklinCovey's *The 7 Habits of Highly Effective People* explains that "the deepest need of the human soul is to feel understood." Think of when you've been treated with empathy. It feels good to be understood, and it feels extraordinary when someone really "gets you."

Empathy tends to be reciprocal. When we are treated with empathy, we often respond with empathy. And showing genuine empathy to others makes us feel good, too.

Unfortunately, we often don't feel empathy from the people and organizations whose very business it is to serve us. How often have you walked into a store needing assistance and no one notices you? For example, the woman behind the pharmacy counter continues a conversation with a coworker while you stand there and wait; the employee at the home center walks briskly past as if you don't exist; the guy at the car-rental desk talks on the phone, his eyes shielded so you can't see them while you are left gripping the counter, staring at him for one, two, five, minutes (which feel like hours).

As customers, how often do we feel that service providers not only can't see us, but can't hear us either. Perhaps our dinner order comes out wrong, or we ask for a drink that never arrives. We have to repeat ourselves over and over again on a customer-service call or are forced to call out "Hello?" when no one is attending to us.

It's not that these frontline people don't have empathy. We believe most do, because we're all born with empathy. Scientists even know which part of the brain is the empathy center: It's called the *subgenual anterior cingulate*, and it actually lights up when we see, for example, someone get poked with a needle. It makes us gasp because, for a nanosecond, we feel the other person's pain. This part of the brain also lights up when we do something nice for another person. The human brain actually feels for other people. Of course, some people have more empathy than others, but we all respond to another's emotional state. As we work to improve our team's customer loyalty, the concept of empathy doesn't need to be taught—everyone already has it. Instead, we need to help our team focus on the mindset and skills that allow us to show empathy for and share the feelings of our customers *more often*.

One skill that allows us to exhibit empathy with our customers is prioritization of our customers above other important tasks. Many of us have an army of people giving us things to do. We have goals, quotas, tasks. We are endlessly pulled off one task to do another. We get caught up in a whirlwind of demands, some of them contradictory. In an imaginary dialogue with a customer, one employee told it straight: "It's not that I don't want to help you. I'm sure you're a nice person who didn't mean to bother me. But if given a choice between ticking you off (a stranger I don't know) or my boss (who will call me incompetent, lazy, etc., if I don't get my inventory done), I choose to tick you off instead. Ultimately, my boss signs my paycheck, and you're a face I will forget in a few hours."

Is the employee wrong to think this way? We once heard a colleague say, "If it weren't for these pesky customers, I could actually get some work done." It wasn't entirely a joke.

Most employees really want to be helpful but are just so busy with conflicting priorities that they struggle to give empathy the time it deserves. Harvard Business School professor Clayton Christensen provided a broader view:

> **Many products fail because companies develop them from the wrong perspective. Companies focus too much on what they want to sell their customers rather than what those customers really need. What's missing is empathy—a deep understanding of what problems customers are trying to solve.**

If we want loyal customers, empathy cannot be one priority among many. It has to be at the top of our list—not just for the frontline customer-service team but for every person in the organization, including people who work on product development, systems design, manufacturing, sales, marketing, or billing.

WHAT DOES EMPATHY LOOK LIKE?

Kanyon Hillaire is a Safelite AutoGlass technician in the northwestern United States. He is also a member of the Native American

Lummi Nation. "They are a great people, very loving," Kanyon says of his culture. Every morning, Kanyon phones his customers to talk about repairing the glass in their automobiles. One day, he learned that one of his appointments that day was a hearing-impaired individual, and he was immediately concerned about that person. He felt empathy. Customers must understand what they can expect during the appointment, how long it will take, and when it's safe to drive the car once the repairs are done. Kanyon was concerned whether he could communicate these things adequately to his customer.

Kanyon contacted a friend who knew American Sign Language and asked her to record a video message for the customer on his smartphone. "I could have written everything down for my customer," Kanyon explained. "But have you ever seen someone after you've spoken to them in their native language? If not, try it some time. Just learn a little bit, and that person becomes more relaxed, and they feel more comfortable. For me, customer service is more than just doing a good job. When the customer saw the video, he was nodding his head and laughing with joy, and so grateful. The walls between us did fall." The customer understood and appreciatively followed Kanyon's instructions.

Kanyon's story has made the rounds on social media. Marketing expert Greg Vitarelli saw it and wrote: "The other day I came upon something completely unexpected that brought me to tears. . . . It came from a very unusual place—an auto-glass company. The honest-to-goodness humanity on display is breathtaking. . . . Kanyon is truly a role model for customer-service professionals." Kanyon's mindset drives him to exhibit empathy with every customer. Let's look more deeply at some of the key points of this story.

For me, customer service is more than just doing a good job. Many would be satisfied with "doing a good job"; clearly, Kanyon is not. There's more. It's about breaking down walls between people and truly understanding one another. It's about making customers feel appreciated, understood, and even giving them joy.

Have you ever seen someone after you've spoken to them in their native language? What is your customer's "native language," or rather, what is unique about how they communicate with you and others? We show empathy when we speak their language, and when we do so in a way that respects their culture, thinking, and way of life.

Honest-to-goodness humanity on display. It would be easy to just do the windshield repair for the deaf customer, as for any other customer, and call it good. Some of us would go a little further and jot down written notes to share with the individual who can't hear. Kanyon delivers even more: He brings "honest-to-goodness humanity." Kanyon's behavior has a profound impact on his customers and on the success of his auto-glass company.

"But I'm busy. I have a job to do," you say. That's true. All of us have a job to do. And a critical part of that job is showing empathy to our customers, both inside and outside the organization.

In practical terms, empathy looks like this: When someone approaches, we set aside what we're doing, close our laptop, put our phone away, and focus on that person. We listen to them with our eyes and ears. Does it take time to show empathy? Yes, and no. It certainly requires effort, but it begins with a mindset (or, perhaps better said, a "heartset"). And often we'll pay a heavier price in time, effort, and money for not showing empathy.

APATHY

The opposite of empathy is apathy, which literally means "no feeling," or not caring. It only takes a small gesture to signal apathy. A bored glance or a sigh of annoyance communicates to a customer that she isn't important. Customers can feel apathy from an organization through a frontline employee's behavior, as well as a number of other sources, for example, a poorly designed website, long hold times on the support line, a complicated bill, or a confusing check-in procedure at a hospital or hotel.

We've experienced apathetic service, and we've likely all felt apathetic at times as well. Apathy can come from life events that leave us demoralized or hopeless. It can come from exhaustion or boredom with our routines. Empathy starts with us. We don't need to be a manager to be an empathy leader and have empathy for those around us.

Stephen R. Covey said: "People are very tender, very sensitive inside. I don't believe age or experience makes much difference. Inside, even within the most toughened and calloused exteriors, are the tender feelings and emotions of the heart." The surest way to reach an apathetic heart is empathy from us. Simply connect and listen to others, behaviors we will discuss in the following chapters.

In the effort to make customers think they care, some organizations set up systems and processes designed to give a feeling of personal service, but these are not rooted in empathy. It works like this. Imagine we call the cable company and tell them our television signal is on the blink.

The wooden voice on the other end says: "First, Mr. Johnson, let me thank you for being our customer for, uh, the last two years. We know you have a choice of providers, and we really appreciate your business. May I take just a moment to express to you how sincerely sorry I am to hear that you are not receiving a signal. I certainly understand how inconvenient it must be. I get frustrated, too, when this sort of thing happens to me, Mr. Johnson. So to be sure I under-stand, the purpose of your call is to get technical support because your signal is not working. Is that right?"

No one is impressed with scripted responses and phony attempts at empathy, yet we encounter these frequently—from the automatic "Find everything?" at the grocery-store checkout to the robotic "How are you feeling today?" from a too-busy doctor in the hos-pital. Researchers from the Corporate Executive Board describe these interactions as "generic service":

> **[One of the] biggest driver[s] of disloyalty is "generic service"—when the customer feels like the rep is treating them like a number, making no attempt to personalize the experience whatsoever. As customers, we know the pain of this sort of treatment all too well. The disinterested recitation of policy. The halfhearted offers of empathy. The scripted thanks for our loyalty. It's enough to make our blood boil.[1]**

Rebekah Bernard, an author and doctor, said: "Empathy is the ability to give the impression that you understand and care. . . . You don't actually have to feel it, you just have to show it." We couldn't disagree more. Empathy is an emotion—a way we connect with others. Maybe "fake it till you make it" can be useful in some circum-stances, but nothing replaces true caring and compassion. Imagine the difference between working on a team with plastic smiles and programmed responses with one that authentically smiles and initiates friendly conversation. Which team do we want to be on? Which team do we want to assist us when we need help?

Employees working with a suggested script can still deliver the message in a way that exhibits genuine empathy, the first principle for earning customer loyalty. On a recent JetBlue flight, we witnessed the flight attendant remind passengers about the rules for keeping seat belts fastened after landing and during taxiing in a way that showed real caring and concern for the passengers and not in the harsh, biting tone we sometimes experience on other airlines.

Here's another story about empathy from a customer-service representative: Our friend bought a new mobile phone for his wife. He was told the monthly service fee would be around $30. He had some negative experiences with cell-phone billing and really wanted to make sure that the $30 was accurate, so he verified the fee with the salesperson twice, wrote it down, and even asked the salesperson to sign it. It would definitely be no more than $30 per month. You can imagine his frustration when the next month's bill came in at $136.

He absolutely dreaded making the customer-service call to the company. When he finally got a person on the phone (after ten minutes of electronic routing and rerouting), he simply asked, "Can I tell you my story?" Fortunately, the agent said "Yes" in a kind voice, heard him out, and solved the problem within minutes. He admits to being a little dazed at that kind of empathy. "It was so unexpected," he said, his voice full of emotion. Like our friend, what people really want is for customer support to understand their story.

HIDDEN STORIES

Empathy is the road to a person's real story—a story that is often hidden from view. Remember the characters in your favorite comic book? Above each character's head was a thought or speech bubble with their words, thoughts, and feelings. You knew exactly what was in the character's head and heart. Imagine for a moment that you could see into the mind of your customers. It doesn't matter what kind of business you're in or the customers you have. As people walk past you, what do you think their hidden stories are?

- An elderly woman who suffered from clinical depression for fifty years.

- A man dressed in mechanic's clothes, tainted with grease. His only daughter is about to graduate from college, the first one in the family to do so.

- A husband whose wife just lost her job. He's going to be the only provider for a while.

- A businesswoman who earned a huge job promotion.

- A man dressed in a business suit who just dropped off his only son at rehab . . . again.

- Two siblings together for a long-anticipated family reunion.

- A young couple expecting a child after a previous miscarriage.

- A young man whose girlfriend just accepted his marriage proposal.

Notice we didn't tell you what kind of product or service they're looking for. Just for a moment, put that aside. How would knowing what's on their mind make a difference in the way you serve them? Their hidden stories shape what they need from us—maybe comfort, support, celebration, or compassion. Knowing their stories enables us to serve our customers much better.

The young couple expecting a baby—what brings them to our store? Do we have a special sale on newborn diapers? Empathy might lead us to provide the couple with a handful of coupons to help them out with their baby budget. And if the worst happens again and there is no baby, are we ready to take the product back quietly with no hassle and send them a heartfelt card in the mail? The newly engaged guy—what brings him to our door? What's he looking for? This man has visions of a new family, maybe a new home, a new car, a new life. What can we do to help him realize his dreams?

It may take time to learn the hidden story of someone we see regularly. In other cases, we have only minutes, or even seconds, to discover where a customer is coming from. Our ability to learn someone's hidden story begins with simple observation—by "reading" the other person's eyes and manner and by listening not just to words but to tone of voice. Sometimes we know a person's story by a glance. A workshop participant told us this story:

> **My family and I saved a long time for this vacation. Our flight arrived late at night, and we stood at the airport curb waiting for the hotel shuttle bus to take us to our hotel. It didn't come. And it didn't come. I rang them and they kept saying they'd be right there, but after nearly thirty minutes, the bus hadn't shown up. We were exhausted from a full day of travel, the kids were cranky, and my wife and I were beyond irritated and were starting to get nervous. Then a shuttle bus from**

> another hotel chain pulled up at the curb. The driver gave us a cheerful grin and asked, "Are you staying at my hotel?" "No," we replied, "we're staying at Hotel XYZ." The driver said, "Jump in. I'll take you to Hotel XYZ." I was surprised and delighted. The driver took us to a competitor's hotel. Guess where I now stay whenever I go on a business trip.

Just a glimpse at that tired, distraught family stranded on the curb told the shuttle driver the whole story. And that's all it took for him to exercise a little empathy. Did it cost him? Yes, he had to go a little out of his way. What did it earn him? Potentially, a customer for life, and no doubt the feeling that comes from making someone else's life a little better.

LEADER APPLICATION—THE PRINCIPLE OF EMPATHY

As we shared in Chapter 1, frontline customer-facing employees are often the least-trained, least-valued, and lowest-paid people in the organization. Some are working more than one job, going to school, or straining to hold a family together. With a little empathy, it's easy to see why someone may not be investing all of his or her energies into the organization's key performance indicators.

A leader dealing with apathetic associates often experiences real frustration with an inability to spark empathy. Pep talks, threats, raises, promotions, and rallying cries can only get us so far. So, what's the real solution to a team's lack of empathy? More empathy from the leader. The power of empathy applies just as much to our team members as it does to our customers. FranklinCovey teaches:

> Always treat your employees exactly as you want them to treat your best customers. You can buy a person's hand, but you can't buy his heart. His heart is where his enthusiasm is, his loyalty is. You can buy his back, but you can't buy his brain. That's where his creativity is, his ingenuity, his resourcefulness.

Take a look at team members and what matters to them:

- Sam loves music and is training for his first marathon.
- Maria is going to night classes at the technology center.

- Jack is a cat person and lives in a loft with a rooftop garden.
- Fatima is a part-time yoga instructor and loves to cook.

How might these facts influence their leader's behavior? The extraordinary manager of this team knew Sam really loved music and running, so she occasionally picked up gift cards for him to purchase songs online. She remembered to text him on the day of his marathon to wish him luck and later congratulated him on finishing.

Do we know the stories of our team members? Do we know what their lives are like? What keeps them awake at night? What they dream of? How their families are doing?

A friend told us this story about a small business he once owned:

> I had two employees, Keith and Randy, who were stock clerks just out of high school. They both were sarcastic, impolite, and brash. They would roll their eyes and occasionally laugh at me. They both did the work just fine, but their rudeness was hard to take. Managing Keith, in particular, was tough for me. I thought of myself as a good employer, and I tried hard to get him to change his attitude, but he would laugh me off and continue on the same way. One day I'd had it. I very calmly invited Keith into my office, handed him what I owed him, and told him to go home. I fired him on the spot.
>
> Randy was just as bad-mannered as Keith, but he didn't bother me nearly as much. I had known Randy since childhood and had watched him grow up. I knew him as a little boy whose father was somewhat abusive. I knew him as a playmate to my own kids. I knew that he suffered from severe asthma, a condition that would eventually take his life. I liked his upbeat smile, his quick wit.
>
> One day I put my arm around Randy and thanked him for a job well done. I had done this many times before, but this time he smiled back and gave me a little punch in the arm. I felt connected to Randy. You see, I knew Randy's story, about the trying life he led, about his hopes and dreams. I didn't know Keith's story. In retrospect, I wish I would have taken the time to get to know him.

Stories change hearts. When we know the stories of our team members, when we know their hearts, it can change ours.

There are two ways to create a team with empathy. One is to lead your team there. The other is to hire people who exhibit empathy in their actions. We recommend doing both.

LEADING YOUR TEAM

Focusing a team on empathy starts with the leader. Whether you are the formal leader or not, ask yourself if you are a model of empathy.

Dr. Fred Kiel, whose life's work is understanding how character affects job performance, said, "When it comes to running a business, self-involved, bottom-line-driven leaders rarely deliver the goods." If you're not naturally empathic, you can't sit back and say, "That's just the way I am," and expect to deliver good performance. A lack of empathy breeds the natural consequence of a lack of loyalty. Nobody is loyal to a person who is uncaring. So, it's to your advantage to develop empathy.

You may feel that you just aren't a naturally empathic person, and that this "warm and fuzzy" stuff is for the birds. Don't be discouraged. Dr. Kiel's response to those who say their character is set and that it can't change is: "Yes, it can. I'm firm in that conviction because I've seen many adults successfully take on the challenge of improving their character. Not only that, I've seen how much happier, more satisfying and successful their lives have become as a result."

We overcome our own empathy deficit by intentionally shifting our mindset and by choosing to soften our heart and connect with others. Observe others and discover their hidden stories—the tired shopper; the guy with a complaint; the dad with the bored, crying child; the laid-off worker; the woman cleaning the restrooms. If we focus on shifting our mindset and practicing this first principle of loyalty, we will see the results empathy brings. Continue to do this, and it becomes second nature; it becomes a habit. As leaders, our behavior becomes the behavior our team embraces. We communicate the values of our team in our actions.

Here are a few tips that can help us all create a culture of empathy.

Ask yourself whether empathy is a principle you want to embrace. When you greet someone, is it a heartfelt greeting or a cold, quick nod? Do you show the same kind of empathy both to your customers and your team? There's no point in creating a culture that talks about empathy if you don't really believe in it. If you are or can become an empathic person, and stand for that principle, people will follow you.

Put yourself into their stories. When you're working with customers and employees, try to think about when you've been in their situation. As you observe people, try to figure out what their hidden story might be.

Don't get distracted. If you're writing a text message to one person while talking with another, neither one is getting your best. You need to give your full attention to the customer or employee in front of you if you want to earn that person's loyalty.

HIRING NEW TEAM MEMBERS

If you are involved in hiring, look for people who are naturally gifted with empathy. Researchers call highly empathic people "integrators" because they are good at bringing people together and building relationships. According to biologist Helen Fisher, the brains of these people are influenced a little more than others by what's called the estrogen/oxytocin system. Although one might think this is more prevalent in females, it's not tied to gender.

To recognize an integrator, watch for people who have a record of strong relationships—who are trusting and sensitive to another's feelings. They connect quickly with people. They are diplomatic, good at facilitating consensus, and tend to have exceptional verbal and social skills. In interviewing candidates, observe how well they connect with you and others in the interview process. Note how they talk about past customer experiences and how they express their feelings about their relationships.

TWO PRACTICES OF EMPATHIC PEOPLE

To show empathy to another person, there are two key behaviors or practices we need to focus on:

- Making a genuine human connection
- Listening to learn

We will study these in depth in the next two chapters. Empathic behaviors can be learned and taught, so use the huddle agenda below to direct a meaningful conversation about empathy with your team. And as your team works toward increasing empathy, be sure you recognize and reward the interactions that reflect empathy. Call them out, congratulate your team members for their efforts, and spotlight the success stories.

HUDDLE 2—THE NEED FOR EMPATHY

Empathy is the ability to identify with and understand another's situation or feelings.

1. **CELEBRATE**

   Celebrate someone who created a customer promoter.

2. **LEARN**

   Discuss the following questions:

   a. How does it feel when we are treated with *empathy*?

   b. How does it feel to be treated with *apathy*?

   c. When is it *really important* for us to show empathy?

   d. How can we show empathy even when we are busy?

3. **COMMIT**

   Show empathy to a customer or coworker.

4. **SCHEDULE FOLLOW-UP**

   Huddle 3 date/time? Who will lead?

CHAPTER 3

MAKE A GENUINE HUMAN CONNECTION

"ONLY CONNECT."
—E. M. FORSTER

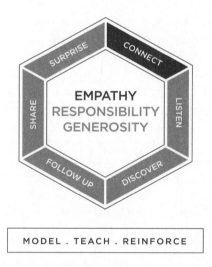

MODEL . TEACH . REINFORCE

Yasir was a sixteen-year-old boy heading out the door for his first job interview. He lived alone with his mom, an immigrant struggling to make a new life for herself and her son. His mother stopped him: "You cannot go to the interview without a tie on." But the boy didn't own a tie and had never even tied a tie. His mother gave him a little money and sent him to the store.

The nervous teen walked into the store, found the men's department, and started searching through the ties for a clip-on. A tall,
friendly man in a red vest came up to him. "What's up?" he asked
kindly. Yasir explained.

"Well, we don't carry clip-on ties, but we've got a lot of nice
regular ties here, all prices. Would you be interested in one of these?"

Yasir looked down at the floor and finally said, "I don't know how
to tie a regular tie."

"I'll show you," said the pleasant guy in the red vest. He selected a
tie that Yasir liked and then instructed him carefully in the science of
putting it on. As he did so, he asked Yasir about the job interview and
gave him pointers on how to succeed at getting his first job. "Look the
boss in the eye and shake hands firmly."

He and Yasir practiced tying the tie and shaking hands and making
eye contact. They attracted the attention of two other employees in
red vests who eagerly pitched in their own advice: "Remember to
speak up. You need to look and sound confident."

While this was going on, another customer was watching.
Touched by the scene, she took a picture with her cell phone and
posted it on social media. Within hours, the picture and the story of
Yasir had gone viral around the world. Yasir didn't find out until after
he had successfully landed the job. The local media interviewed him
and his mother, and they ended up on the television news.

"They could've just sold my son a tie, but they took the time,
helped him tie the tie, and treated my son with dignity and respect,"
the mom said, her voice trembling. "And that's not all—they gave
him real-world advice to help him get the job."

Yasir was amazed at the attention. "After their advice, I got
my confidence back. I was calm, cool, and collected. Usually only
friends or family do that kind of stuff—not strangers you've never met
before." In an alternate scenario, the sales associate would have asked
Yasir if he could help him, then could have quickly dismissed Yasir
with a "Sorry, we don't carry clip-on ties." But in this store, the red
vests stand for something important. The folks who wear them have
a high standard of service. They show empathy and make a genuine
human connection with customers.

Is there any question that Yasir and his mother are now loyal customers? And the woman who took the picture? What about the tens
of thousands of people who saw the red-vest team at work on social
media and television?

WHAT A GENUINE HUMAN CONNECTION LOOKS LIKE

Sandy shares this example: "The other day as I was leaving the corner grocery store, a young worker looked directly at me, smiled, and cheerfully said, 'Thank you for coming!' *Thank you for coming?* I thought. *Like this is a party or something?* I smiled back and said, 'Thank you.' It was a little thing, just a spark of human connection, but somehow I felt uplifted and a lot better about my neighborhood store."

Showing empathy for someone else starts by making a connection with him or her. A genuine connection promotes a feeling of belonging, of acceptance. When we lack these feelings of acceptance, we experience "social pain." The pain caused by a snub or a cold shoulder is as real as physical pain. D. H. Lawrence used the word *annihilated* to describe the feeling of being disconnected from other people. We've all felt moments of alienation.

Some are skeptical and assume people only connect with others in order to gain something or profit from them. But this assumption is lacking. Connection with other people is its own reward.

Shawn shares how simple a warm, human connection can be: "I stopped to pay a bridge toll—never my favorite duty—but my short interaction with the toll-booth operator, fifteen seconds in duration, left me saying out loud to myself as I drove away, 'That was remarkable!' The booth operator, in just a few seconds, made a human connection. I don't remember the words he said, but I do remember how he made me *feel*. The brief encounter left me grateful I had taken that particular route. It doesn't take much to make a warm human connection, and it costs nothing. We all crave it. We even need it. But we get it so rarely."

COUNTERFEIT CONNECTION

As we study the practices that build empathy, we should also consider the "counterfeits" of these practices. A counterfeit practice is like counterfeit money. At a quick glance, it might look real; but closer inspection reveals that it is only an imitation. The counterfeit to a genuine human connection might be feigned interest, intrusion without empathy, or following a script with disinterest. Counterfeit behaviors sneak into organizations as leaders create systems and processes aimed at increasing customer satisfaction without acknowledging the need for genuine connections with customers.

For example, hospitals invest significant money on consultants who provide scripts and checklists to boost satisfaction scores: "An entire industry has sprouted, encouraging hospitals to waste precious dollars on expensive consultants claiming to provide scripts or other resources that boost satisfaction scores. Some institutions have even hired actors to rehearse the scripts with nurses. In Massachusetts, a medical/surgical nurse told the *Boston Globe* that the scripting made her feel like a 'Stepford nurse,' and wondered whether patients would notice that their nurses used identical phrasing. She's right to be concerned. Great nurses are warm, funny, personal, or genuine—and requiring memorized scripts places a needless obstacle in their path."[1] You might be familiar with the adjective "Stepford," which comes from a novel about smiling robots with no feelings or thoughts of their own.

Using these scripts and checklists, service people deliver a canned "Have a nice day," or "Thank you for shopping with us," and as customers, we feel that these are counterfeits. Many service people don't think about these throwaway phrases. We believe the young guy in the corner store—the one who sincerely said, "Thank you for coming," to Sandy—wasn't counterfeiting. He was connecting.

A growing body of research tells us that influence with a customer starts with genuine connection. Just a few signals—a friendly nod or a smile or a wave—can show people they are welcome and we'll be glad to serve them. First impressions matter a lot. People decide quickly whether we are someone they can connect with on a human level and whether we are competent. If we are cold or unapproachable, we immediately risk losing the opportunity for loyalty in our customers. They might find us competent, but we still won't earn their loyalty. The key is to connect warmly with *everyone*. Remember Yasir and his search for a tie? Certainly, he didn't appear to be a big-spending, high-powered customer when he walked into the store as a sixteen-year-old. And yet, the store team didn't hesitate to treat Yasir with as much warmth as one of their most loyal customers.

WHY AREN'T WE CONNECTING?

When we identified genuine human connection as an essential component to earning loyalty, we immediately wondered why the natural connection we all appreciate doesn't happen more often. We began to identify the obstacles that prevent connection. We found there are many, and they are growing.

Think about your most manic days at work. We're talking car-rental counter at a busy airport, lunchtime rush at your favorite restaurant, closing the books at year-end in the finance department, emergency room at a large urban hospital, DMV on the last day of the month—phones ringing, impatient customers, and overworked teammates. How can we possibly make a warm, genuine human connection in situations like these? The number of demands and requests on our time can quickly become the reason we avoid connecting with others. We're just *too busy*. And yet, as we mentioned above, connection can be made with a glance or a word. Being too busy is a poor excuse. Our ability to connect—even on a crazy, busy day—is driven by an understanding that connecting with our customers is an important part of our job.

Another hurdle that is making human connection more difficult is technology. We check ourselves in for a flight, check ourselves out at the grocery store, and do more of our banking and shopping online. We get stuff done by clicking. While many of us appreciate the convenience and cost savings, the expanding use of technology can present challenges in connecting personally with our customers.

Forward-thinking high-tech companies understand the power of human connection, especially when something goes wrong and only a conversation with a human being can resolve it. We've had many personal experiences with Amazon, Apple, and Southwest Airlines where the people on the other end of the phone line, at the Genius Bar, or at the ticket counter did an excellent job in connecting with us in a warm, friendly manner to resolve our issues.

Consider how Lamoda, a Russian online retailer that offers next-day delivery of more than nine hundred brands of men's and women's apparel, is making a genuine human connection. After someone places an order—and more than a million do each year—a Lamoda fashion consultant brings it to your door. He or she gives you a few minutes to try the items on, offers fashion advice, and takes your payment if you're satisfied (or returns part or all of the order if you're not). And while we love the convenience Lamoda provides, you can certainly make a warm human connection remotely and less expensively than coming to someone's door. Sandy shares this example:

One morning, my Keurig coffee machine stopped working. It was early, and I was tired and anxious for a cup of java. The last thing I felt like doing was dialing a call center and

> **potentially being put on hold and transferred and getting frustrated. But that was not the experience I had with Keurig. When I called, the nicest woman answered the phone. I could hear in her tone and her words that she wanted to help me. She had strong empathy for my situation and patiently walked me through each step of the process needed to fix my machine. She never made me feel like it was a problem for her to wait for the machine to do the next step in the repair process. She was so genuine. She wanted me to get my hot cup of coffee as much as I did.**

A car-rental executive (not from Enterprise, National, or Alamo) recently told Sandy about his commitment to take their people completely out of the car-rental process. We heard a customer-experience leader in a major corporation say that customer loyalty is "the result of integrated technology systems that can crunch actionable data-driven insights to create relevant and meaningful customer experiences." We don't want to downplay technology, but we know that simple connection buys more loyalty than any "integrated technology system" can, especially when the customer has a problem and needs to talk with a human being to solve it. The founder of Enterprise Rent-A-Car frequently pointed out, "All rental-car companies have cars, branches, and people. What sets us apart is our people!"

Ultimately, making a genuine connection begins with our mindset. We all need and appreciate connection. If we adopt the mindset that connection matters, that it is a priority, we see people in front of us instead of problems. We see human beings, not hassles. We connect with our eyes, our words, and our heart. This connection can happen in an instant. When we have busy days, we still acknowledge those waiting with an apologetic glance or a quick, sincere "I'm so sorry you're having to wait." We soften our voice, make eye contact, and feel the connection ourselves. No matter how busy we are, we let individuals know that *we* know they are there and that they matter to us.

Having the wrong mindset is an obstacle to connecting. "I'm not a warm person," you might say. "I'd rather just focus on getting my job done." When we shift our mindset to value human connection and the benefit it has on ourselves and others, we prioritize our work differently. Not only do we make time to connect with everyone, we make it our most important task of the day. It becomes our job. The choice to connect with others is just that—a choice. We've always been impressed by this thought from the great psychologist Viktor Frankl:

> **Forces beyond your control can take away everything you possess except one thing, your freedom to choose how you will respond to the situation. You cannot control what happens to you in life, but you can always control what you will feel and do about what happens to you.[2]**

In other words, we get to choose how we feel. Nothing—not the weather, the news, or the auditors from the head office—can dictate to us how we will feel today. That's *our* decision. So let's bring our natural empathy and desire to connect to the surface. The people around us are real human beings; they have dignity and they deserve the best we can give. Each one has a hidden story that would fill us with compassion and allow us to connect if we knew what it was.

And while we are talking about the benefits of connection to loyalty, we can't emphasize enough the benefit connection has on ourselves. A reflected smile or the reciprocation of a few kind words inevitably brightens our day as well. And there is science behind all this: Connecting with others in an affable way increases oxytocin, a hormone associated with calmness and closeness. Too much stress, on the other hand, inhibits oxytocin. So the less kindness we show to others, the more stressed we actually become.

HOW DO WE MAKE A *GENUINE* HUMAN CONNECTION WITH EVERYBODY?

Once you decide to make genuine human connections, there are five behaviors that come naturally and are easy to do:

1. Smile and greet others with a warm welcome.

2. Observe, then serve.

3. Connect warmly with your eyes.

4. Acknowledge others.

5. Be available, but don't hover.

SMILE AND GREET OTHERS
WITH A WARM WELCOME

Our friend Gordon Wilson managed one of the top Apple Stores in the United States and emphasized this rule with his team: "Approach customers with a personalized, warm welcome." Notice that there isn't a script the retail associates need to follow. Everyone who enters an Apple Store gets that warm welcome at the door. At first, Gordon tried to hire "magnetic personalities" for this position. But, he says:

> I soon found out that anybody could handle it. People think Apple Stores hire nerdy, techy people only, but that's not so. At least in my store, I came to believe that just about anyone could be effective at Apple. The issue was never so much with their personalities as it was with mine. If the manager is the kind of person who can love the customers, it becomes contagious.

Apple goes a little further than most to make that human connection. When you enter the store, the greeter makes a note of what you're wearing as she takes down your name and your reason for coming in. Later, when a "specialist"—a sales associate—takes over from the greeter, she or he already knows who you are and why you've come. They call you by name. This is pretty remarkable when you consider the thousands of people visiting each Apple Store every day.

OBSERVE, THEN SERVE

One day, a mom and her young son walk into a sporting-goods store. "Simon, are you really sure you want to play soccer this year?" Mom asks, a worried, hesitant tone in her voice.

The boy looks nervous. "Sure, Mom."

Curtis, the floor manager, breaks away from his conversation with Sue, who is a newly hired sales associate. Curtis greets the mom: "Good morning! Welcome to SportStuff. How may I help you?"

The mom replies, "Well, my son Simon is just starting to play soccer this coming Saturday, so he needs some equipment. I'm not really sure—"

Interrupting, Curtis says cheerfully: "I know exactly what he needs: cleats, shin guards, and a uniform. And how about a new ball?

We'll get him set up just right. Sue, would you like to take care of these folks?" Sue nods confidently and leads the mom and her son toward the soccer equipment.

What do you think of this interaction? Curtis is positive and considerate, he takes time to coach his staff, and he wants to help his customers. But as Sherlock Holmes used to say to Watson, "You *see*, but you do not *observe*." Curtis isn't observant enough to catch on to the customer's story, which means he doesn't really know how to serve the customer. He tries to *serve* before he *observes*.

Let's observe. It wasn't an anonymous child who came into his store. It was a little boy named Simon, and when Simon woke up that morning, he felt anxious. While he badly wants to be on the soccer team, he's nervous about whether he'll be good enough, whether he'll get hurt, and whether the other kids will like him. Pretty big stuff for an eight-year-old. How do we know all of this? We are not mind readers, but anyone with ordinary observational powers can pretty much tell what's going on in Simon's mind just by watching him.

And look at Mom. She has never done this before. She has all the same worries as Simon. She brought Simon to this particular sporting-goods store because it's close to home. There are other stores. At this point, the only relationship she has with SportStuff is transactional—which most stores are fine with, unless they want truly loyal customers.

If Curtis saw his task as earning the loyalty of his customers so they won't want to shop anywhere else, he would approach the situation differently. So let's give Curtis a chance to be "Empathic Curtis." We'll rewind and start the story over again.

One day, a mom and her young son walk into a sporting-goods store and have an anxious dialogue about playing soccer that year. Empathic Curtis, the floor manager, carefully observes the mother and son as they come through the door. He motions to Sue, his new hire, to follow him.

Empathic Curtis greets the mom: "Good morning! Welcome to SportStuff. What's going on today?"

The mom replies: "Well, my son Simon is just starting to play soccer this coming Saturday, so he needs some equipment. I'm not really sure what kind of equipment to get, although they gave me this list." She shows Curtis an image on her phone, which he studies for a moment, nodding.

Then Empathic Curtis squats down to be at eye level with the little boy. "Hi, Simon. I'm Curtis. Have you ever played soccer before?"

Uncertain and visibly nervous, Simon replies: "I already have my own ball. I kick it around the yard."

"You know, Simon, I started playing soccer when I was about your age, and I remember feeling a little worried. I didn't want to get hurt by all the kicking, so I got some really good shin guards, like these." He shows Simon how to fix them around his shins.

"And I wanted to run as fast I could," Empathic Curtis goes on, opening a shoebox. "These shoes have what are called cleats on the soles to grab the ground and keep you from falling when you run." Simon takes the shoes in his hands and looks delighted with them.

Empathic Curtis smiles. "But you know, Simon, the fun part of soccer is being on a great team. You can help them, and they'll help you. So you'll want to look like part of the team with a cool green uniform. Let's go find one." Now comfortable with Curtis, Simon eagerly follows him to the clothing racks.

The mom whispers to Sue: "I didn't want to say, but Simon's been feeling really anxious about soccer. I think he's going to feel a lot better now." They watch as Curtis shows Simon, now wearing a crisp, oversized soccer shirt, how to kick a soccer ball.

"I think he's going to be fine," Sue says with a smile.

Now Curtis is doing his *real* job, which is enriching a little boy's life. And in doing that, he's also making friends who will come back again and again. In a town full of sporting-goods stores, where do you think Mom will shop in the future? And all her friends will, too, once she tells them about the wonderful man at SportStuff who was so good with little Simon.

What did Empathic Curtis do differently the second time around? He talked to the boy at his own level; he addressed the boy's—and the mom's—worries by explaining the value of the products and demonstrated how to use them. All good practices. But Curtis could not have done this job without careful observation and empathy. Just by the boy's body language and the look on his face, Curtis could tell a lot about his little client's hidden story.

The idea is to *observe, then serve*. What unexpressed emotions do you sense? What is the customer's demeanor? Sad? Rushed? Eager? Hesitant? Curious? Overwhelmed? What about their tone of voice? Angry? Excited? Pleading? Worried? Ho-hum? It doesn't take a lot of skill to see through a customer's manner to the story behind it all. But if you want *loyal* customers, you'll be watchful. You'll pick up these nuances of behavior and allow your empathy and connection to kick in while you match your own behavior to theirs.

CONNECT WARMLY WITH YOUR EYES

As humans, we connect immediately with someone who gives us a warm look. Every customer-service expert rightly tells us to look the customer in the eye. It is intuitive that eye contact is essential to making a human connection, and while it's common sense, it's not always common practice. Further, if we want to make a genuine connection, we can soften our gaze and smile to add warmth. Think about those situations where we tend to lose eye contact. If we keep a customer waiting too long, we're losing eye contact. If we spend too much time fumbling around with products or paperwork, we're losing eye contact. What if we're connecting with customers online—on email, chat, messaging, or the telephone? What does "eye contact" mean then?

There's a lot of research that supports how difficult it is to connect online. "The increasing use of electronic services, or e-services, raises questions concerning the extent to which the 'relationship quality-customer loyalty' link holds in an e-service context," as one scholar put it. Online, the equivalent of "eye contact" is a warm, calm, respectful tone of voice and doing what we promise. One older gentleman who ordered some window blinds online praised the "eye contact" practiced by the firm he dealt with, even though he never met anyone at the company face-to-face:

> **Your employee, Sarah, made "eye contact." She advised me that my blinds were on their way and checked to see if I was happy with them after they arrived. When I discovered they weren't quite right, she kept up that contact, everything from the remake to the shipping with a tracking number to your website and to the personal notes you sent me. You kept "eye contact" with me. It's great to see a quality business still thriving in this crazy economy. It's because you do what you do, and you have people like Sarah making "eye contact."[3]**

Experts tell us that, without building robust emotional bonds with customers, organizations won't be able to enhance customer loyalty. Customer connection—or making customers feel good every time they contact the organization—should replace the antiquated "customer-relationship management" agenda. With every customer interaction comes a chance to look them in the eye and build a closer connection.[4] "Eye contact is way more intimate than words will ever be," says Indian author Faraaz Kazi.

How consistent is your team in building connection through warm eye contact? Some people have a kind of reflex to avoid eye contact with others. If you need to, work at overcoming that reflex and practice giving everyone a warm look in the eye.

ACKNOWLEDGE OTHERS

One evening, a man went to a restaurant and stood at the reception desk where the host was chatting with a couple of waiters. He smiled at them, cleared his throat, and waited. After a minute or so, he realized that somehow he had become invisible. The conversation among the staff was not particularly urgent—they were joking around about something—but it was clearly far more absorbing than the fact that a willing customer was standing there in plain sight waiting for service.

At last he spoke up. "Excuse me, but do you have a table available?" The three of them looked up in surprise and glanced at one another. It must have taken them a second or two to remember they were at work, but at length he finally got his table. You may have experienced this non-service yourself on occasion. Associates who ignore the customers, rush past people without even a nod or a smile, or keep them on hold for too long are chipping away at loyalty one little bit at a time.

Should any customer ever be invisible? If guests were to come to your home, would you simply fail to notice they were there? How *attentive* is your team to the customers who pay you to help them out? Elizabeth Muenich, manager of customer service for the city of St. Paul, Minnesota, shared in a conversation how she has made it a top priority for her team to acknowledge and connect with every one of their customers.

> It has given my staff permission to take a few extra moments in the workday to interact with our contractors, business owners, and our residents. In a world where interfacing with regulatory agencies is perceived as very difficult and filled with red tape and struggles . . . our staff is making human connections every day to create collaborative partnerships instead of conflict and separation within our city.

We've been in busy places where a first-rate service person can connect with a half-dozen customers at once. Sometimes all it takes is a smile and a sincere "I'll be right with you" to connect with the customer. It doesn't require much, really. We can't show empathy or connect with customers if we don't acknowledge that they're standing right in front of us.

BE AVAILABLE, BUT DON'T HOVER

Once we've made a genuine human connection with our customers, we'll often support them throughout the "journey" with our organization. This doesn't necessarily require our constant undivided attention, nor does it mean smothering them or hovering. In one furniture store we know, customers bump into eager salespeople at every turn. Rather than building loyalty, the store has an infamous reputation for smothering people. Judging how much help to give customers versus how much space they need can be tricky at times. The best practice is to "make yourself available." Make warm eye contact, smile, and greet customers. Then let them know you're available by saying, "I'll be right over here if you need anything." Periodically, check in to see if they have any questions, but generally be aware of physical proximity and avoid making them uncomfortable by being in their personal space.

For phone or virtual support, "making yourself available" means checking in periodically while you are researching an issue, making sure your customer knows your name, and that they have the capability to contact you directly if they need additional support. Invite them to reach out to you if they need anything further.

LEADER APPLICATION—THE PRACTICE OF MAKING A GENUINE HUMAN CONNECTION

Pete Matthews was the manager of a large chain store in Canada, and his first year in this position was miserable. He thought his job was to manage numbers and increase performance. But after a while, he realized that wasn't the whole story.

> I was totally focused on the KPIs (Key Performance Indicators)— ROI, CR, CCC, CUR, OFCT, DIFOT—I was responsible for about twenty-five different sets of initials. Every day, I was checking items off a huge checklist and continually ragging

on my department heads when their numbers on this, that, and the other didn't meet expectations.

After about half a year of this, I realized something. I didn't know anyone. I had dozens of employees I couldn't name. Here I'd been working with my staff for months, and I couldn't tell you anything about them. And customers? I knew nothing about them either. Without an employee badge, I wouldn't know a customer from a staffer. I had been counting numbers and ratios for so long that I had totally failed to make the human connection.

One morning, I gathered the department heads and held up a copy of the KPIs. "I've worried myself and you to death about these numbers long enough. They're not getting any better, but they're not getting any worse either. So I'm going to stop worrying about them." I tossed the papers into the trash—it was overdramatic, but it was my way of declaring independence from the KPIs.

"From now on, we're going to get to know each other— and our customers. I figure if we are loyal to each other and treat each other right, those numbers will take care of themselves." Well, everyone laughed. Some didn't believe me at first. But I stopped talking about the KPIs so much and spent my time making friends with the staff and with our customers. I asked all about their families and their likes and dislikes and got to know them pretty well. The customers were a little surprised that the store manager would roam up to them and just pass the time of day, but only a few weeks later, I could recognize a big percentage of them and knew a lot of their names.

The most rewarding thing of all, though, was my association with my team. We became friends—in some cases, dear friends—and years after I left that job, I still consider working with that team one of the best experiences of my life.

Oh—and the KPIs got better the whole time.

Pete's employee loyalty to his work team spilled over into a more personal connection with their customers. Of course, Pete didn't really ignore the KPIs; but of all the numbers, he was most proud of the customer-loyalty number that went up steadily during the three years he managed the store. It turns out that his change of heart was contagious.

As leaders, we sometimes work in organizations that try to force human connection through scripts and checklists, streamlining processes in a way that can *limit* genuine connection. Most team members will comply with expectations, but it's a golden few who will go beyond to actually make a connection that earns loyalty. Doubling down on efforts to force connection further creates a culture of compliance. If we instead focus on the benefit of connecting with customers, model this behavior as we connect with our employees, and trust our employees to make connections naturally, we create a culture that values genuine human connection. The Southwest Airlines' flight attendant who sings the before-takeoff announcement not only delivers the important safety information, but does so in a way that makes genuine human connections.

HUDDLE 3–MAKE A GENUINE HUMAN CONNECTION

Let people know you care and are there to help.

1. **CELEBRATE**

   Celebrate someone who showed empathy to a customer or coworker.

2. **LEARN**

   Discuss the following questions:

   a. How do some people pretend to make a genuine connection?

   b. What gets in the way of us connecting with everyone?

   c. Which of the connection guidelines do we need to improve on?

   d. How can we acknowledge people even when we're busy?

3. **COMMIT**

   Make a genuine human connection with a customer.

4. **SCHEDULE FOLLOW-UP**

   Huddle 4 date/time? Who will lead?

CHAPTER 4

LISTEN TO LEARN THE HIDDEN STORY

—

"IF WE WOULD ONLY LISTEN WITH THE SAME PASSION
THAT WE FEEL ABOUT WANTING TO BE HEARD."
—DR. HARRIET LERNER

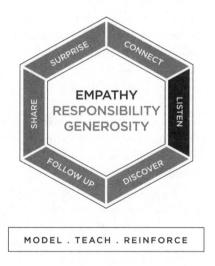

One day, our friend developed a strange pain in his scalp that felt like someone was cutting through his head with a piece of wire. He called his doctor, but she wasn't available. He was advised to head for the local urgent-care clinic. At the clinic, our friend found himself surrounded by fellow patients with fevers, coughs, and stomachaches.

Everybody looked miserable. At the reception desk, a stern woman interrogated him about his insurance and told him to "take a seat."

A suffering hour later, a sharp voice called his name. He followed a man in surgical greens into a cold little room. "How are you doing?" the man asked briskly. Our friend explained his experience—that he had woken up with a knifelike pain across the top of his head. He'd had a long history of sinus trouble and suspected the old complaint was emerging again. He even knew the name of the infection he had lived with forever: *haemophilus influenzae*. But the green man wasn't interested in any of this. "I'm not the doctor," he interrupted as our friend was explaining his history. "I just take your blood pressure."

Let's pause the story for a moment. How are you feeling about the empathy shown to our friend so far by the reception desk and the medical assistant in surgical greens? Were there any genuine human connections? Was anyone sincerely interested in listening to learn his story?

The story continues.

Following the blood-pressure check, the green man disappeared without a word and left our friend in the tiny, freezing room for another half hour. When a doctor finally appeared, he was incredibly hurried, as you might imagine, with the backlog of patients. After listening for just a moment, the doctor declared that our friend had shingles and ripped a prescription off of his pad, sending our friend on his way.

Strike three—no empathy from the three people our friend encountered at the urgent-"care" clinic. Sure, they were all busy. But how long does it take to make a warm human connection? And what was the cost of not listening to learn?

Our friend filled the prescription and took the medicine, but it didn't help the pain he was experiencing. The doctor didn't take time to understand his story about a history of sinus trouble. Unpredictably, a few weeks later, he was taken to the hospital with an acute sinus abscess that threatened his brain. This urgent-care clinic failed to show our friend any empathy, and also failed in its responsibility to solve his real problem, which is the subject of Chapter 6.

We believe the serious oversight by this doctor was neither driven by incompetence nor ill intent. The doctor, like many of us, was confronted with the nearly impossible task of juggling too many demands and was simply trying to be efficient. There is a downside to efficiency when we're working with human beings—we may neglect to take time to empathize and really listen.

Dr. Joshua Kosowsky, who teaches medicine at Harvard University, says, "The key to helping patients is to try and arrive together at a diagnosis. And the key to diagnosis is right in front of us: It lies in our patient and his or her *story*, not in a recipe that reduces a patient to a symptom or two."[1] As organizations work to standardize customer service in order to become more efficient, they risk becoming less empathic. In pursuit of efficiency, we all have the tendency to stop listening to individual customers and just assume most have the same need.

As author Michael Bassey Johnson said, "A good listener is one who always pays attention, not to gain, but to learn." So the skill we are focused on here is not only listening to hear, but also *listening to learn*.

Organizations pay a high price for not listening. According to author and consultant Dan Bobinski: "Millions of dollars are lost every day in organizations simply because of poor listening. . . . Poor listening leads to assumptions and misunderstandings. These lead to errors, ineffective decisions, and /or costly mistakes. On a personal level, poor listening leads to hurt feelings and a loss of team cohesion. This deteriorates trust and weakens communication even further."[2]

SIS International Research (New York City) reports that 70 percent of small to mid-size businesses are losing money due to ineffective listening and communication. They estimate that a business with one hundred employees, for example, spends an average downtime of seventeen hours a week clarifying communication, which translates to an annual cost of more than $500,000 each year.[3]

On a personal level, when we fail to listen, we not only miss the opportunity to show empathy and earn loyalty by connecting and learning from someone's story, but we also fail to fulfill what we at FranklinCovey teach is the greatest human need: to feel understood. With so much at stake, it's easy to see how listening to learn is vital to earning loyalty.

WHAT DOES "LISTENING TO LEARN" LOOK LIKE?

As we shared in Chapter 2, every customer has a hidden story. By making a genuine human connection and listening to learn, we uncover their story, which then allows us to feel and convey empathy.

You may be thinking, "We don't have time to listen to every customer's story," and of course there's some truth to that. But at Franklin-Covey we teach, "With people, fast is slow and slow is fast." If we are sincerely interested in earning someone's loyalty, it often pays to slow down just a little bit and listen to learn.

Of course, this requires the awareness of when to do it. Think of how many people wander around a business, much longer than they'd like, because they can't find what they're looking for—in this instance, shoelaces. Perhaps the customer is too timid to approach the customer-service person (ironically, because that person looks too busy to be of service). When the customer works up the gumption to ask his or her question, the customer-service person might look genuinely surprised and think, *Where do we keep shoelaces, anyway?*

But what if you, the empathic service person, see this customer wandering in a daze, and stop to ask: "Hello! What can I help you find?"

"Oh, I'm looking for shoelaces."

"Great, let me show you where we keep them. What puts you in the market for shoelaces?" This might seem like a ridiculous thing to ask, but it actually gives you the opportunity to listen to learn.

"My child has broken his shoelaces—again—and has an important game this afternoon."

You could introduce him to the new elastic laces you've just added to inventory. More important, during your short walk together over to the aisle with shoelaces, you could say: "Well, that's exciting. You must be so proud of your son. What position does he play?"

"He's a pitcher, but he hasn't gotten much playing time lately. He hurt his arm last week."

"I am so sorry to hear that. With a big game coming up, I am sure that is frustrating for him."

This is the skill of *listening to learn*. When you do this, you learn more about the other person's story, and doing so enables you to show empathy. Listening to learn is not just a mechanical skill. It's the result of *really wanting* to learn, of *caring* enough about another person to connect and listen for a moment.

Of course, "Listen to the customer" is one of the most common clichés in business. Everybody knows we should listen to our customers. Often, however, we hear someone talk, but we react without learning what's beneath their words.

Customer: "I'm looking for shoelaces."

You: "Sure! Shoelaces are on Aisle 12."

There. You listened. But you didn't listen *to learn*.

Many of us think of ourselves as above-average listeners. We've learned how to listen in management training or in marriage counseling or by reading a brilliant business book. We've learned the skill of active listening, where we fully concentrate, focus intensely, and give facial and verbal cues as we process what is said. Active listening is an important and useful skill, but if our real intent isn't to understand the other person, then it comes across as fake, and people see through it.

Listening to learn comes from a heartfelt desire to truly understand other people. The more we understand, the more we can help them; the more we help them, the more loyal they become. The mindset shift to empathy that we discussed in Chapter 2 will naturally drive the behavior of listening to learn, because we want to connect to understand another person's story. The listening-to-learn behavior is rooted in the principle of empathy because it is about fully understanding and empathizing with the *story* of another. We define "story" as the person's emotions, knowledge, experience, and point of view—the narrative behind the need. In Chapter 6, you'll learn how we further bring needs to the surface by making sure the solution/outcome is *really* what the other person is seeking.

COUNTERFEIT LISTENING

Loyalty does not arise if we pretend to listen, or half-listen, while waiting for our turn to talk. It's easy to spot when people aren't listening to us. They talk over us, interrupt us, or simply dismiss what we're saying. In customer service, any of these behaviors are just flat-out rude. But this is not what we mean by counterfeit listening.

Instead, counterfeit listening occurs when we pretend to listen, but other things are running through our head. We counterfeit listen when we are thinking about our response rather than trying to really understand; or when we assume we already know what another person is thinking and, therefore, don't need to give our full attention when we are nodding and checking our phone screen at the same time or talking and texting simultaneously.

The word *phubbing* was coined in 2012 to describe the habit of snubbing someone in favor of using our mobile phone. James A.

Roberts, a marketing professor at Baylor University, conducted a study
among 450 U.S. adults and found that 46 percent of respondents said
their partners phubbed them, and 23 percent said it caused issues in
their relationship. Truthfully, when we get busy and are under stress,
counterfeit-listening behaviors, like phubbing, are easy to slip into.

WHY AREN'T WE LISTENING TO LEARN?

Christine Riordan made this observation:

> **Too often, leaders seek to take command, direct
> conversations, talk too much, or worry about what they will
> say next in defense or rebuttal. Additionally, leaders can react
> quickly, get distracted during a conversation, or fail to make
> the time to listen to others. Finally, leaders can be ineffective
> at listening if they are competitive; if they multitask, such as
> reading emails or text messages; or if they let their egos get
> in the way of listening to what others have to say.[4]**

Riordan identifies three reasons why many people aren't listening
to learn:

- We think listening isn't work.
- We're too distracted to listen.
- We let our ego get in the way.

WE THINK LISTENING ISN'T WORK

If the surveys are accurate, listening to learn is not a focus because:
"It's too time-consuming, it isn't productive, I have more important
things to do than to stand here listening to you." According to com-
munity building experts, we mistakenly think that "to listen is to
retreat from productivity."[5]

Do we think that if we spend too much time listening to people,
we're "wasting time" and we're not being "productive"? Well, maybe,
if we only measure productivity by how busy we are. If we look
at the metrics we're responsible for, "hours spent listening" is most
likely not one of them. As long as we define productivity only by the
numbers we track, then we will continue to be *insanely* busy, with an
emphasis on *insane*.

If improving customer and employee loyalty is really important to us, then listening to learn may be some of the most important work we do.

WE'RE TOO DISTRACTED TO LISTEN

We are so sidetracked by mobile phones, tablets, and other tech devices that we fail to hear what's being said. When we consider all the pinging, dinging, and ringing paraphernalia in nearly any situation, it's not surprising that people complain they aren't heard. One researcher who has studied communication in a hospital setting notes this:

> **Patients ask why the doctors and nurses don't listen: "I've answered the same question five times, but they keep asking it." Nurses wonder why doctors and administrators don't listen, and doctors and administrators wonder how to get nurses to listen. We know it is important for patients and nurses to "speak up"—yet how can we ensure someone is listening?[6]**

Certainly, it's tricky to balance all the things coming at us from many sources at once. We're talking to someone and the phone rings. What do we do? There's not one simple "right" answer to this—the circumstances vary, as do company policies and personal comfort. In making this judgment call, remember the mindset of empathy and the skill of making a genuine connection. A quick "Thank you for calling. May I please put you on hold while I assist another customer?" might strike a good balance. It's when the distraction becomes the focus that we're in trouble.

WE LET OUR EGO GET IN THE WAY

Paul Bennett is the senior creative officer of the famous innovation firm IDEO. When Paul became a manager, he said, "I assumed that the world was more interested in me than I was in it, so I spent most of my time talking, usually in a quite uninformed way, about whatever I thought, rushing to be clever, thinking about what I was going to say to someone rather than listening to what they were saying to me."

Dr. Lisa Sanders of Yale School of Medicine says, "Most patients have a story to tell . . . but the odds are overwhelming that the patient won't get much of an opportunity to tell that story. Doctors frequently interrupt their patients before they get to tell their full story." Research shows doctors listen on average about sixteen seconds before breaking in. Is this due to ego? Trying to be efficient? Because they're overworked?

Dr. William Osler was a highly respected physician and is often referred to as "the father of modern medicine" because he was the first professor of medicine to insist that medical students leave the lecture room and talk to actual patients. He said, "It is much more important to know what kind of patient has the disease than to know what kind of disease the patient has." What a wonderful sentiment that applies to all of us on our journey to increasing loyalty.

HOW DO WE LISTEN TO LEARN?

There are four things you can do to listen to learn:

- Stay silent until the person has finished talking.
- Listen with your ears, eyes, and heart.
- Don't worry about how to answer—focus on understanding.
- Rephrase what was said and check for understanding.

STAY SILENT UNTIL THE PERSON HAS FINISHED TALKING

Sandy shares that his dad frequently advises family members to use their ears and mouth in the proportion with which they were given. Easy to say and hard to do, especially if emotion is building in the conversation. This could be anger, excitement, frustration, or delight. Keeping quiet until the other person has completely finished talking takes discipline. But it can be mastered with practice, and it goes a long way toward communicating to others that you genuinely care about their thoughts and feelings.

LISTEN WITH YOUR EARS, EYES, AND HEART

We've talked about the importance of the eyes in making a warm human connection. When we say "listen with your heart," we mean you grasp the *feeling* as well as the *content* of what is said, and this behavior is rooted in empathy. The Chinese character for the verb "to listen" contains the symbols for the ears, the eyes, and the heart. If you listen only with the ears, you get content but you might not get feeling. If you also listen with the eyes and the heart, you will hear what is said as well as how it is meant. Together, these symbols signify that to truly listen is to give undivided attention to the other person and arrive at true understanding.

Ears

Eyes

Undivided
Attention

Heart

FranklinCovey teaches: "When you really listen with a pure desire to understand, you'll be amazed how fast people will open up. They want to open up, layer upon layer—it's like peeling an onion."

A friend of ours shared the experience of trying to get to Boston for an important meeting:

> Caught in terrible traffic early one morning, I arrived at the gate, breathless, seconds after the door closed on my nonstop cross-country flight. It is, of course, airline policy that no one be admitted once the door is closed.
>
> "Sorry, sir, the gate's been closed."
>
> "But the plane is sitting right there. You just barely closed it. Please, can't you give me a break? I've got to be in Boston this afternoon for a crucial meeting."
>
> "No, sir," the uniformed shirt said with finality. "I've been calling your name for ten minutes. I can't help it if you're not here on time." He was merciless, and I was desperate.
>
> "When can you get me on a flight to Boston?" I anxiously asked.
>
> "Not until eleven o'clock." It was three hours away. "And you'll have to connect through Chicago." The situation kept getting worse. Wordlessly, he stared at his computer and finally got me set up for the next flight. As I walked away in misery to wait for three hours, I could have used a little

empathy. Instead, I heard the gate attendant shout coldly at me, "You just left your wallet here. Unless you want me to spend all your money, you probably ought to pick it up." I walked back, picked up my wallet, and sat, exasperated, until the next flight took off.

When I arrived in Chicago, I realized my next flight was delayed due to deteriorating weather and it was, therefore, very unlikely that I would arrive in Boston in time for my meeting. I went to the airline's help desk to see if there were any other options to get me to Boston for at least some of the meeting. I queued up for what seemed like ages. As I began to explain my situation to the help-desk person, he literally put his hand up in my face like a stop sign. "Can't help you," he said and then shrugged and turned to the next customer in line. I was sick about missing my meeting and frantically decided to try another airline.

At Airline 2, the help desk was staffed by a pleasant woman who listened to my story. "It sounds like you've had an awful morning. Let me see what I can do." She checked her system and found that—alas!—there was no way to get me to Boston in time for the meeting.

"However, sir," she said, brightening up, "our passenger lounge is right over there. Although we can't get you physically to your meeting, we can set you up to attend it remotely. It's quiet in the lounge, and we're fully equipped to connect you to your colleagues in Boston."

"Oh, I'm not a premium customer," I interjected, thinking there was a misunderstanding.

"I know," she said, smiling. "It's our pleasure to help you connect to your meeting."

She went even further. She canceled my original flight and booked me on a return trip for that night. I was able to participate in the meeting I couldn't miss and then had a leisurely flight home.

The woman at Airline 2 could have blown our friend off just like the guys at Airline 1. She could have said, "There's no way," just as the others did and then turned her back on him. Instead, she chose to have empathy, to connect, and to listen. She listened with her ears, eyes, and heart. Only through taking a moment to listen was she able to show some empathy and help our friend solve his problem. Think about what it cost her—a few minutes of her time? What would it cost you and your coworkers to practice this kind of empathy? You won't be surprised to learn that, since this experience, our friend has avoided Airline 1 and flies Airline 2 whenever possible. That one experience created a loyal customer. Certainly worth a few minutes to listen to learn about a situation.

DON'T WORRY ABOUT HOW TO ANSWER— FOCUS ON UNDERSTANDING

So much of the advice one receives on how to listen includes keeping quiet and focusing on understanding the other person. Of course, this is great counsel, particularly when we're having a hard time opening lines of communication. In building customer loyalty, we also want to get others to talk, because that's the only way we can learn their hidden stories. Whether it's their social conditioning, shyness, time pressure, or distraction, customers don't often chatter during simple transactions. Imagine a transaction where the standard "Did you find everything you were looking for?" was answered with "No. I'm looking for a better life. I'm looking for happiness. I'm looking for that spark I lost years ago." OK, so maybe that's a little extreme, but we actually do want a true response from our customer.

According to the prominent psychiatrist Dr. Mark Goulston, an expert on listening, active listening is more about getting people to talk than about staying silent:

> **I had this assumption that it was all about reining in your own feelings and any distractions so you could be fully present. But actually [it's about] getting other people to talk, to share the information with you that maybe is in their head but that they just weren't disclosing before. . . . The key is helping them to talk about what's most important, critical, and urgent to them.**[7]

We love this formula: "What is most important, critical, and urgent to a person?" If we can find that out, we can truly meet our customers' needs.

So how do we create opportunities for people to talk? It's usually pretty simple. Ask them a question. In fact, asking the right question will not only spark conversation, it will allow us to listen to learn.

There are three categories of questions we can use to spark conversations with our customers: simple, open, and burning questions.

Ask simple, friendly questions. "What's the occasion?" "What are you thinking of doing with this [product]?" "What are you working on?" Or just plain old "What's going on?" Make the question as easy and sincere as you can in order to get the story.

Ask open questions, not closed or yes/no questions. If you ask yes/no questions, that's all you'll get: yes or no. "Did you find what you were looking for?" is a yes/no question. It doesn't invite conversation, unless the answer is no—and it rarely is. Don't ask, "Got a project going?" That's a yes/no. Instead, ask, "What kind of project are you doing?" Now you're into a conversation.

Ask burning questions. Burning questions are those that are likely to be important, critical, and urgent. For example, "What problem are you trying to solve?" "What are you hoping to accomplish?" "What's the biggest challenge you're having with your deck?" "Could you share a few more of your thoughts about this?" "Here's what I suggest. What do you think?"

Once we ask questions, we'll need to see the conversation through. Asking a throwaway question when we don't care about the answer will decrease customer loyalty, rather than build it. Serving customers isn't about making idle conversation. Customers typically don't want idle chitchat. But they deeply appreciate our willingness to listen to show empathy.

REPHRASE WHAT WAS SAID
AND CHECK FOR UNDERSTANDING

We want to get people talking. And once we open the conversation, it makes no sense to shut it down after a few seconds. We're listening to learn, so instead of imposing a solution on the person right away, continue the conversation through *Empathic Listening*. Empathic Listening is the skill of reflecting both the content of the person's concern and the feeling he or she has about it. This process has the incredible ability to uncover what's really on someone's mind, and it's also a critical skill when there's emotion in the conversation.

Reflecting what the other person says in your own words will give insight into both feelings and content of what's being said. A customer could come to you angry or excited about a purchase. A colleague could come to you frightened or enthusiastic about an upcoming change in the business. Observe how they feel, really listen to what they are saying. Then, reflect what they've said in your own words. You might choose to reflect only the emotion, or only the content, of what they've said, or you might reflect both. One example of Empathic Listening is illustrated below:

EMPATHIC LISTENING RESPONSES

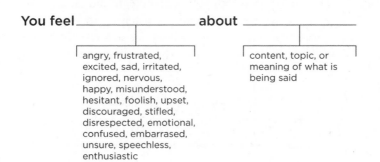

You feel _____ about _____

angry, frustrated, excited, sad, irritated, ignored, nervous, happy, misunderstood, hesitant, foolish, upset, discouraged, stifled, disrespected, emotional, confused, embarrased, unsure, speechless, enthusiastic

content, topic, or meaning of what is being said

Let's play this out in an example: A customer has just purchased an item from you, and the next day it goes on sale for 50 percent off. She's livid. "I could have gotten this for half price if I'd waited a few hours. You must have known it was going on sale. This is ridiculous!"

Getting defensive and quoting policy at her won't create loyalty. Instead, say, "You're frustrated that you didn't get the sale price." Now, that response may sound strange at first, but it validates the customer. It signals to her that we understand where she's coming from and that we're not going to discredit the way she feels. Also, it keeps her talking until the problem is disclosed and the emotion abates. Finally, it relieves our own anxiety if we recognize and validate, instead of drawing a battle line we have to defend. Further, we're not thinking about what we're going to say in response; we're only focused on understanding her.

From there, how you resolve the concern is determined by any number of factors—policy, timing, circumstance, and so on—but solving the problem is secondary to understanding through the skill of Empathic Listening.

We might be hesitant to enter a conversation with an associate or a customer because we are uncertain where the conversation will go. Is this customer going to dump details of his or her divorce on me?

Will my colleague bring up yet another problem? Will the person in front of me ask me a question I have no clue how to answer? With regard to loyalty, the richer the conversation, the more loyalty is built. Instead of worrying about the potential outcome, just ask the question and see where it goes.

Listening gets inside other people's frame of reference. We look out through it, we see the world the way they see the world, we understand their paradigm, we understand how they feel. If our goal is to build and maintain loyalty, we must empathize, connect, and listen to learn the concerns or needs of others. The skill of listening to learn allows us to gain rich information about our customers and team members. We're better able to help them and increase the trust in our relationships.

LEADER APPLICATION— THE PRACTICE OF LISTENING TO LEARN

Employee surveys are full of feedback like this:

- "No one seems to know what's going on."

- "Nobody listens to me."

- "Our leaders only pretend to listen. They've already decided what to do."

- "I have no idea what my manager is thinking."

As leaders in our own organization and consultants to others, we've never encountered an organization where people say: "Oh, communication? Yeah, we've got that nailed. We're already brilliant at that." In fact, 91 percent of employees say their bosses don't listen to them.[8] The impact of not listening is massive—not only in terms of culture, employee loyalty, and employee engagement, but there's a price we pay in innovation, collaboration, and problem solving when our people talk and we don't hear them.

Being a leader is a unique experience. The executive team looks to you to solve problems. Your team looks to you for answers. We're paid to get the job done, and there's an assumption that we have all the answers. So it's easy to default into *telling* rather than *listening*. But listening, as we've discussed in this chapter, is the key to understanding our employees and customers and an essential step to earning their loyalty.

HUDDLE 4—LISTEN TO LEARN THE HIDDEN STORY

Listen to understand people without worrying or thinking about how to answer.

1. **CELEBRATE**

   Celebrate someone who made a genuine connection with a customer.

2. **LEARN**

   Discuss the following questions:

   a. What are we really trying to learn by listening?

   b. Which of the "Listen to Learn" guidelines do we need to improve on?

   c. What does it mean to "listen with our ears, eyes, and heart"?

   d. How do we check for understanding without solving the problem?

3. **COMMIT**

   Listen to learn a customer's hidden story.

4. **SCHEDULE FOLLOW-UP**

   Huddle 5 date/time? Who will lead?

PART
THREE

THE PRINCIPLE
OF RESPONSIBILITY

CHAPTER 5

THE NEED FOR RESPONSIBILITY

"OWNERSHIP: A COMMITMENT OF THE HEART, HEAD, AND HANDS TO FIX THE PROBLEM."
—JOHN G. MILLER, AUTHOR OF *QBQ!*

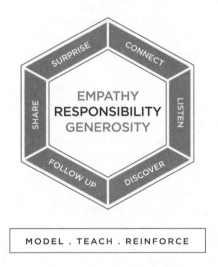

Responsibility is the second of the Three Core Loyalty Principles. The best businesses are ready to take responsibility for our problems, our needs, and their relationship with us. They meet us at the door. They return a text immediately. They answer the phone. They empathize with us, do the job we need done, then follow up to make sure it was done right. All of this conveys that we are important to them, and it goes a long way toward earning our loyalty.

Empathy is the principle of understanding other people so they feel valued, while responsibility is taking ownership for the actions that follow such an understanding to help people achieve their goals. Showing empathy without demonstrating responsibility is unlikely to earn another's loyalty.

Think of times when customer-service people really took responsibility for you. What did they do to show they were responsible? How did it make you feel? Now think about a time when you took responsibility for another's needs. How did it feel to solve a problem for someone who was depending on you? Like showing empathy, taking responsibility benefits both the receiver and the giver. When we give support to others, it reduces the activity in the threat-related regions of our brains and may be an effective way to reduce stress.[1] When we take responsibility for helping others, our own stress levels drop!

WHAT DOES RESPONSIBILITY LOOK LIKE?

John G. Miller, author of *QBQ! The Question Behind the Question*, brilliantly defined responsibility this way: "It's ownership: A commitment of the heart, head, and hands to fix the problem and never again affix the blame."[2] A commitment of the *heart* means we care about our customer's problem. A commitment of the *head* means we know what to do about it. And a commitment of the *hands* means we are willing to do what's necessary to solve it. That's responsibility. A friend shares this experience:

> One day I was eating a quick lunch in New York City not far from our publisher's office. I was about to meet him for the first time and of course wanted to make a good impression. In a hurry to eat, I sat down too hastily and dumped my meatball sandwich onto my shirt. Now covered with greasy tomato sauce and Parmesan cheese, I looked at my watch and realized the meeting was in twenty minutes. I couldn't go into the office of a big New York publishing house dripping meatballs, so I frantically searched for a place where I could buy a new shirt. Fortunately, there was a small men's clothing store just a few doors away. The salesman

immediately understood my problem. "Don't worry," he said with a wonderful New York accent. "I guarantee you will make your meeting in a brand-new shirt."

He measured me quickly and found a beautiful shirt my size that was just right, but it was wrinkled. "I can press it in two minutes." I was anxious, but the salesman seemed to set a speed record for ironing a shirt and then buttoning it on me. Smiling broadly, he led me into the street, patted me on the back, and directed me where to go for my meeting. I actually arrived a couple of minutes early! I still love that shirt salesman in New York and talk about him wherever I go. As soon as he saw my predicament, he took total charge of the situation. No long explanations were required, no hassles, no waiting, no passing me from one salesman to another, no going to find an employee lower on the totem pole to press my shirt. He "owned" my problem and solved it with minimum effort on my part and maximum efficiency on his.

What an amazing example of responsibility in action. It's easy to imagine that the salesperson felt pride and satisfaction as our friend marched down the street toward his meeting.

INDIFFERENCE

Contrast the shirt story above with another story we heard from a client:

I once bought an expensive pair of walking shoes from a boutique that specialized in orthopedically correct shoes. After only a couple of weeks of use, my toes started to protrude through the fabric. I was surprised that the shoes had worn so fast, and I went back to the shop to talk to them about it. The manager was away, but I pointed out the problem to the assistant manager, who looked down at the shoes and shrugged. "Yeah, they'll do that." He turned and walked away. I was stunned. No one had warned me that these high-tech walking shoes were so delicate that you couldn't actually walk in them. The dismissal was as painful as my disappointment in the shoes.

A shrug is the universal sign of indifference. It doesn't have to be an actual shrug—there are many symbolic ways to convey that indifference. An endless telephone hold, getting no response to your email. A shrug, whether literal or figurative, tells customers they are not valued. It's the "not my responsibility" mindset that destroys loyalty. Loyalty requires us to shift our thinking from "not my job" to "it's *all* my job!"

Beyond the shrug of indifference, there are two other ways that we see organizations miss taking responsibility and, therefore, miss the opportunity to build loyalty. First, they focus on touchpoint metrics, and second, they set up what we call "maze systems."

It's common for companies to identify what we call "touchpoints" in the customer relationship—that is, those times when they come into contact with their customers. They measure customer reactions at those touchpoints to arrive at a "customer delight" score. Most of the time, these touchpoint scores are pretty good and, as a result, many companies feel great about their level of customer delight.

But some years ago, researchers at McKinsey ran into a problem with touchpoint measures. They found that overall customer-experience scores run about 40 percent lower than what touchpoint scores indicate.[3] It turns out that touchpoints are only part of the story. The rest of the story? It's what happens when the customer leaves the touchpoint and goes home to his or her new reality.

- The new garden rake loses its head during its first use.

- The new Wi-Fi router only works from inside the closet.

- The cell-phone bill is a third higher than it should have been.

- The bottled salad dressing arrives broken, but to get a refund, it has to be boxed up and sent back (are they serious?).

- It takes hours to figure out the instructions for assembling a kitchen stool.

- The color on the wall looks nothing like the color on the paint chip.

When confronted with these "after the fact" situations, some customers just do their own shrug of indifference. They don't bother to follow up, call for help, or return the item. But let's not be fooled. Perhaps they feel the problem isn't worth fussing about, but this could also be a reflection of what little faith they have in our willingness to take responsibility for their problem. At these critical moments, taking responsibility for customers' issues, needs, challenges, or questions is an excellent opportunity to differentiate our company from others. Research from the Corporate Executive Board concludes that "disloyalty among customers is largely associated with the amount of work—or effort—customers must put forth to get their issues resolved."[4]

Let's use the garden rake and its severed head as an example to explore this further. When the head fell off the rake that was purchased earlier in the day, it added to the effort the customer had to go through to get his work done. Not only does he still have the original work to do, but now he has the added task of either fixing the rake, finding a different tool to use, or heading back to the store. This might seem like a trivial example, but the day it happened was undoubtedly a busy day full of many tasks, only one of which was gardening.

Let's rewind to when the customer first went into the home center. Imagine him walking in and asking where he can find a rake. Now, think of a customer-service person who takes full responsibility for the customer. He might reply, "Sure, I can show you right where they are. We've got a good selection of rakes. Are you looking to rake leaves, or is there something else you'd like to use the rake for?"

In fact, the customer was planning to move a lot of dense soil with the rake, and no doubt needed a more heavy-duty tool for that purpose. Without an in-depth knowledge of rakes, it's easy for the customer to get it wrong. If the customer-service person does an exceptional job of selling a standard leaf rake, they might get a perfect "touchpoint" score, and the customer would likely leave the store happy. But it's later that afternoon, knee-deep in soil, that the customer's loyalty is built or lost.

"Just take the stupid rake back" is undoubtedly running through some of our minds. That *would* be the natural thing to do if it were convenient, and if the customer has confidence that the home store will make it hassle-free and painless to return the broken one and get the right rake. But if there's any doubt about how he'll be treated, the customer may just throw the rake away and try shopping at another home store in the future.

According to the CEB, taking responsibility for your customers means that you "find new ways to get rid of the hassles, the hurdles, the extra customer effort that leads to disloyalty."[5] Companies that are fastest and easiest to work with often win the highest loyalty scores.

Zappos, for example, scores twice as high as traditional apparel competitors primarily for "saving time" and "avoiding hassles."[6] Zappos was founded by a man frustrated because he was stonewalled at local shoe stores when he went looking for his favorite lightweight shoes. Responsible firms are always looking for ways to relieve the customer's stress level.

In addition to a misguided focus on touchpoint customer-service metrics (rather than the customer's whole journey with your organization to complete a task), many companies create maze systems in an effort to increase efficiency. These systems may be set up with the intent to get customers to the right department, but they feel like mazes. And while it's fun to run through a garden maze, it's not as fun to stumble through the mazes companies create to "help" their customers solve problems. For example, there are policies for deciding when to escalate a problem to a manager who, in turn, is given a checklist before escalating to an even higher manager. We all know firsthand how aggravating this can be. "Why can't the person I'm talking to now solve my problem?" we ask.

Our friend Breck tells this story about the "maze" he got caught in:

> I was on vacation in London and tried to buy an expensive multi-day Underground pass from a machine, which promptly ate my money but neglected to give me the pass. I found a gate agent, who took me into an office and had me fill out four (that's 4!) pages of paperwork. I was then told that I had to take the papers across London to the Piccadilly station where the "Customer-Service Office" was located. Arriving at Piccadilly, I found that the office was closed and locked! So I searched around for an agent who referred me to a supervisor, who referred me to yet a higher supervisor, who wandered away and disappeared with the paperwork. A full half hour later, the official at last emerged from a back office and presented me with my money.

Because the first agent wasn't able to help him, Breck was forced to navigate an actual Underground maze and lost nearly two hours of his vacation time. Another frustrating "maze" we're all familiar with is the "phone-menu maze." Phone menus might make routing calls easier for the company, but they universally drive customers *crazy*. According to Boston University researchers, people have hated phone menus for a generation (public opinion is "almost uniformly negative"), but they're still "the most common entrée to customer-service help."[7]

It's natural to wonder, *Are we expecting too much of frontline people by asking them to*:

- Take responsibility for the customer's problem?

- Foresee potential problems customers may have with their products?

- Find an exact fit with each customer's needs?

This depends on how we define the job of our people. If we see their role as taking responsibility and solving problems, then meeting the needs of each customer will come naturally.

Fred Reichheld said that customer-loyalty scores actually measure how much we are enriching the lives of others. "As corny as it sounds," he says, "a company's success is truly defined by how many lives the company enriches."[8] So, how focused are you and your team on enriching the lives of others?

And while we may not be able to influence our entire organization's systems, we *can* individually choose to take responsibility for our customers. We agree with author and teacher David Freemantle: "The act of personalizing service requires . . . personal ownership of each interaction with a customer and thus accepting responsibility for developing and progressing the relationship."[9] Putting this in our words, we need to take personal ownership of the customer—*personally.*

Jeff Haden is a writer for *Inc.* magazine and an amateur cyclist. For months, he'd been looking forward to a big race. The day before the race, his prize bicycle broke. The repair-shop guy said he could fix it. "When do you need it?" he asked.

"Tomorrow!" Jeff responded, distraught.

He expected the repairman's response to be, "Not possible." Instead, the repairman asked, "Why do you need it tomorrow?"

After Jeff explained the problem, the repairman replied: "We have a [bike] we're using for test rides, and it's the right frame size for you. It's super light, but it is also designed for endurance and comfort. You could rent it for the day if you want."

"And I did," said Jeff. "Problem solved. I didn't get what I thought I wanted—but I did get what I came for."[10]

That's the key point about responsibility. Customers need to get what they came to us for. If they don't, we're not taking ownership for their problem. "I don't need you to delight me," Jeff is saying. "Just give me some relief!"

Responsibility is one of the most important principles for earning and retaining the loyalty of others. First, take time to empathize, connect with, and listen to your customer. Then, take responsibility for their needs. A client of ours, a cancer survivor, told us about his experience with two very different nurses—one who displayed empathy, connection, listening, and responsibility, and one who did not. Notice the different impact generated by each experience.

> When the nurse standing in front of me told me I had lymph cancer, she went straight into the "protocol" with precision and efficiency: "Here's what you're going to do, what we're going to do, what's next, what you can expect. Do you understand?"
>
> Well, I didn't understand a word. I'd heard nothing after she said the word "cancer." I felt like my stomach had been kicked in and my life was over. I sat numb while the nurse finished up her instructions and left the room. I was shocked, alone, and, frankly, scared.
>
> Another nurse came in the room to take over my case. This second nurse sat down and looked at me. "It's just the worst, isn't it?" And then she listened to me as I choked up and babbled and cried. I could feel that she felt with me. "I'm going to stay with you all the way through this," she said. And she did, week after week. One day during my treatment, I was lying there really depressed when she came in my room carrying scissors and some old magazines and said, "Now cut out all the happy pictures and paste them on construction paper."
>
> I thought, "How stupid," but we did it together and talked and laughed a bit. Then she took me down to the children's ward where we posted the pictures on the walls to cheer up the little kids with cancer. I felt almost human again.

The first nurse was doing her job—and was probably really good at efficiently handling patients—but clearly struggled to feel empathy for the patient and take responsibility for the client's need (which at that moment was to feel comforted). By contrast, the second nurse connected immediately with his overwhelming need. She also recognized that her job was not just medical care but also emotional care. Her kindness, her ingenuity at doing the real job, and her willingness to follow up is what we mean by taking responsibility for the customer.

LEADER APPLICATION—
THE PRINCIPLE OF RESPONSIBILITY

One dictionary definition of responsibility is "the opportunity or ability to act independently and make decisions without authorization." As leaders, it is our responsibility to create a team that is capable and empowered to meet our customers' needs.

Marketing entrepreneur Peter Shankman tells the story of returning to his hotel room after a day of meetings to find a brand-new tube of toothpaste on the bathroom counter. Apparently, he'd left his old, nearly empty tube out and the housekeeper took notice and replaced it. In that hotel, there is no doubt that the leaders create a culture of responsibility and empower their people to take action.

We don't know what the tube of toothpaste cost that hotel. We do know that by giving the housekeeper the responsibility for helping fulfill actual needs, they reap great rewards. In this case, Shankman tweeted a picture of the maid's note, and the hotel staff later told him they had tracked "thousands of dollars" of reservations back to his tweet.

According to Pete Matthews, former manager of several big chain stores, "I always thought it was my failure when an employee came to me with a customer issue. I should've prepared that employee to take care of the customer without involving me." Pete's rule was that any employee should be able to do anything he could do at his level. Although we might be tempted to be the manager who can fix everything, customers don't want to deal with us. It's a hassle. That's why Pete said to his team, "The moment a customer comes to you with a problem, it's your responsibility, nobody else's."

TD Bank tells frontline employees, "It takes one to say yes, but two to say no." In other words, you are empowered to say "yes," and if you feel that you need to say "no" to a customer, please check with your manager first.

You can create teams of highly responsible people through your leadership, and if you hire new team members, you can look to bring on people who naturally take responsibility.

LEADING YOUR TEAM

As managers, we are responsible for responsibility. Our own behavior becomes the standard for our team to follow, and when they see us taking responsibility for customer issues, they will find it easier to do themselves.

Our friend Gordon Wilson, whom we mentioned earlier (see Chapter 3), managed an Apple Store and was a model of taking responsibility. One day he noticed as a customer began to look ill. He kept her in his line of sight so he could assist her if needed. She was leaning against the wall and growing pale; suddenly, she vomited all over the floor. Everyone in the busy store froze, except Gordon. Without hesitation, he saw that the woman was cared for, then grabbed a mop and bucket and started cleaning up. The employees saw this and, of course, they pitched in as well. They knew they were working for a leader who took responsibility himself, and they followed his behavior.

Often the more responsibility we give team members, the more loyal they become to us as leaders. Reflect on a time when you had a leader who trusted you to take responsibility for a job, a need, or a customer. When others trust us, we rise to the occasion. When team members know we trust them with customers, they feel more responsibility to the customer and to us. They become more engaged in their work and in finding solutions. Gallup has found that if our employees are engaged with our business, we're likely to enjoy at least 10 percent higher customer loyalty and 20 percent higher revenues. And if we're in the top quartile of employee engagement, we are on average 21 percent more profitable over bottom-quartile teams.[11]

How far should we trust team members to be responsible for customers? We're not advocating that you hand the new employee the keys to the kingdom and hope he comes through for you. We believe that you have to evaluate the circumstance and the employee, set very clear expectations, equip your team with the resources and structure, then let them do their job. Don't hover, don't double-check every step of the way. In his classic book *The Speed of Trust*, Stephen M. R. Covey points out, "Micromanagers who trust only themselves . . . are demoralizing to work with. They run the high risk of driving away their best and most talented people who simply won't work in a restrictive environment of control."[12]

Sandy shares this story from his experience leading the Enterprise car-rental operation in London, England:

> We held our operational managers responsible for customer service by only promoting those people whose customer-service scores were equal to or above our company-average score. Anxious to get promoted, our managers stayed focused on improving service, or at the very least, maintaining an "average or better" score relative to their peers. Some managers struggling to improve their service offered excuses like: "It's more challenging running a branch in a big city like central London," or "How am I supposed to know how to get better when there's only two survey questions, and we only get twenty-five surveys for my branch each month?"
>
> To ensure our branch managers maintained ownership and responsibility for *their* customer service, I coached their managers—our area and city operational leaders—to avoid the temptation to give them answers and instead to ask questions like:
> • What are you learning from your peers who run similar operations (i.e., they also run a big branch in central London) and have better customer-service scores? What are they doing differently than your team?
> • Why do you think 30 percent of your customers are not completely satisfied?
> • What are you learning as you observe your people interacting with customers?
> • If you want more feedback, why not ask more of your customers, "What, if anything, could we have done better to serve you today?" This enables you to fix the problem with the customer and the employee right away and prevent similar issues.

In our work with many different organizations over the past twenty-five years, we caution senior leaders to never take responsibility for improving service away from the front line. At Franklin-Covey we teach: "No involvement, no commitment!" Unfortunately, we see too many senior leaders fielding long surveys (which customers despise and most refuse to complete) and then relying on data analysts and sophisticated software to *tell* frontline people how to get better.

Asking questions and empowering frontline teams to figure out how to get better takes a few extra steps, but it builds trust, empowerment, and important capabilities in your future leaders.

Here are a few tips for creating a culture of responsibility on your team:

Ask yourself, "Am I a responsible person?" We need to reflect on our own performance, both past and present. Do we take responsibility for our role and our work without shuffling it off onto someone else? Delegation is an important part of any leader's role; we just need to make sure we are delegating the right things. Are we the kind of leaders who can take blame when things go wrong and give credit when things go right?

Step up and take responsibility. Do we do what we expect others to do? Team members are more willing to do any job they're asked to do if they see us doing the same. When they see us clean the floor or carry a customer's purchases to her car, they notice. When they see us take over a shift for a sick staff member or give our hands an extra wash after working with a patient, they will feel better about doing the same. It's important that we truly model the principle of responsibility.

Trust your team. We need to appropriately equip our team with training, resources, systems, and expectations. And then, take a risk. Trust them to do their jobs. Understand that there might be failures. When there are, take time to self-evaluate. Make sure the expectations we set were clear enough, that the resources were available, and that the systems in place aren't sabotaging our team.

HIRING NEW TEAM MEMBERS

Peter Schutz, the former president of Porsche, said, "Hire character, train skill." Some people are intuitively more responsible, and if you can find them, they are good candidates. Researchers said, "For service employees to display customer-oriented behaviors, the organization must first recruit individuals with high levels of conscientiousness."[13] They're out there, and they are essential if you want your team to build customer loyalty.

Biological researcher Helen Fisher calls responsible people "guardians" because we can rely on them to take charge of a situation. "Data and facts and details matter" to them. They guard both your interests and the customer's. They stick with a problem until it's solved.

According to Fisher, the brains of these people are influenced a little more than others by what's called the serotonin system, which makes them more sociable, more team-oriented.

How can we recognize a "guardian"? Watch for people who have a strong sense of obligation to other people and a record of seeing things through. They don't shrug things off or drop the ball. They have good questioning and investigative skills. In the interview process, ask candidates for examples of when they had to solve challenging customer issues. Look for ownership and responsibility in their answers.

TWO PRACTICES OF RESPONSIBLE PEOPLE

There are two key practices that we focus on to build loyalty through responsibility:

- Discover the real job to be done.

- Follow up to strengthen the relationship.

Because these two practices are core to responsibility, we'll spend the next two chapters on them. For now, ask yourself, *What is it that our customers come to us for? What are their needs? What are they trying to accomplish? How good are we at following through on our commitments to them? Do we ever shrug and walk away?*

HUDDLE 5—THE NEED FOR RESPONSIBILITY

Responsibility is taking ownership of what should be done.

1. **CELEBRATE**

   Celebrate someone who learned a customer's hidden story.

2. **LEARN**

   Discuss the following questions:

   a. When did someone take responsibility for *truly* helping you?

   b. What would indifference look like on our team?

   c. In what situations is it *really important* for us to take ownership?

   d. What prevents us from taking responsibility for a customer's needs?

3. **COMMIT**

   Take complete responsibility for a customer's needs.

4. **SCHEDULE FOLLOW-UP**

   Huddle 6 date/time? Who will lead?

CHAPTER 6

DISCOVER THE REAL JOB TO BE DONE

―

> "IF I HAD ASKED CUSTOMERS WHAT THEY WANTED, THEY WOULD HAVE SAID 'FASTER HORSES.'"
> —ATTRIBUTED TO HENRY FORD

Let's imagine working in one of these organizations below. A customer asks—

- Sporting-goods store: *"Can I buy a treadmill?"*
- IT department: *"We need more efficient technology for our offices."*
- Hardware store: *"I need a bigger wrench!"*

- Accounting department: *"Can I get a breakdown of last quarter's revenue by channel?"*

"Of course!" we reply, and we dive right into what the customer needs. We walk him or her to the treadmills, research technology, or start cranking on the spreadsheet. We deliver the goods or service and mark it off our task list like a champ, feeling productive and accomplished. A job well done!

Let's pause for a moment and review where we're at. We began with the need to adopt the Loyalty Leader Mindset based on the Three Core Loyalty Principles. In Chapter 4, we learned how to listen to learn about the other person's story, including his or her emotional state, so we can show empathy and feel what that person is feeling. In looking back to our friend in the urgent-care clinic (see Chapter 4), his story included his history with the sinus infection he had lived with for many years: *haemophilus influenzae.* But because he hadn't been adequately listened to, he was given the wrong diagnosis and course of treatment. His need remained unknown and unmet.

We assume responsibility for the other person's goal or problem by discovering the real job to be done. We may be doing a great job at taking responsibility for the client in the moment, but if we rush to deliver the client's request, it's not entirely clear our solution is aligned to what that person truly needs. Discovering the real job to be done is the functional application that allows us, as responsible people, to make sure people achieve the solution or outcome they are really seeking.

WHAT DOES "DISCOVERING THE REAL JOB TO BE DONE" LOOK LIKE?

Harvard professor Clayton Christensen asks, "Are we too focused on what we want to sell, rather than on what customers actually need?" It's easy to rush to recommend, solve, or sell because we know our products and solutions, and we know how these things solve the needs of our average customer. However, Clayton Christiansen goes on to say, "Customers rarely make buying decisions around what the 'average' customer in their category may do—they often buy things because they find themselves with a problem they would like to solve."[1] So the challenge is that, if we don't know what the problem is, we can't take responsibility for meeting our client's need. This idea is captured in Theodore Levitt's quote: "People don't want to buy a quarter-inch drill. They want a quarter-inch hole."

The "real job to be done" is the end result our customer is trying to achieve. To truly take responsibility for our customers, we need to understand their needs, what their problem is, and what they're trying to accomplish.

One day our friend walked into one of those big electronics stores and was awestruck by the display of speakers hanging from the wall. This wall was *glorious*. The lighting, the colors, the signage, the balance—it was wonderful to behold. It was also totally baffling.

He was looking for some speakers so he could get surround sound to go with his brand-new, 72-inch television, but he knew nothing about sound equipment. All he knew was that he wanted his basement television room to sound like a movie theater. He looked around for some help, but with no one around, he continued to inspect the brilliant wall of speakers—tall thin speakers, short squatty speakers, speakers that looked like shoeboxes and pineapples and golf balls. For all he knew, they *were* shoeboxes, pineapples, and golf balls, but he examined each one with a faux-expert squint until, suddenly, a voice boomed behind him.

"Help you?" a very large man with "Mike" on his name tag asked between chews of his gum. He was a big, bearded, store employee wearing earphones.

"Yes, I'm looking for some speakers for my new television."

"Well, this new Bluetooth sound bar is pretty cool." The giant pointed to a low, wide box that looked like a car bumper with head-lights. "It's wireless and everything."

That sounded good to my friend so he bought it on the spot.

"Cool," Mike repeated, taking my friend's credit card and then set-tling back into whatever he was listening to on his earphones. Excited, my friend opened the speaker the minute he got home. The satiny black box was indeed cool. He took a cursory look at the instruction manual, which was incomprehensible to him, plugged the box into the wall, and turned on his television. Being wireless, the black thing should just start booming away, he thought.

Nothing happened. He sat stunned for a moment before picking up the owner's manual and trying unsuccessfully to make sense of the instructions. He stared at the black box for a while longer and then gave up, deflated.

Over the next few busy days, our friend's family members quizzed him about the "thing" in the basement television room. "What is that thing? How does it work?"

After several weeks, my friend's son pointed to the box and asked him, "What are you going to do with that? Does it even work?"

Reluctant to admit that he was at a loss, he worried about the expense and dreaded the trouble of returning the speaker. He finally decided he had no choice. Our friend boxed up the speaker and carried it all the way into the city and back to the store.

This time he encountered a different employee: a woman with short black hair and a bright smile. "Hi, I'm Francine. That's a nice big box you're carrying. What's going on today?"

"I bought this sound bar for my television, but it doesn't seem to work."

"Oh, I'm sorry to hear that," Francine replied with genuine empathy. "I know how frustrating it is when you buy something you're excited about and it doesn't work. Let's find out how I can help you. Can you walk me through what happened?"

Our friend told her his story.

"Again, I'm really sorry," Francine responded. "And after all that, you even had to lug it all the way back here. Let's see if we can get it right this time. Tell me what you were hoping for in the first place."

"Well, I just wanted fantastic surround sound to go with my new television. You know, booming loud like in a movie theater."

"We've got some great speakers, so I think we can get some that will do that for you. Can you tell me what kind of television you have?" She immediately knew that his particular television wasn't equipped for wireless speakers, so she looked through her products and found an inexpensive wireless transmitter that would enable his television to communicate with the sound bar.

But she didn't stop there. She demonstrated for him on a television set in her store exactly how to install the transmitter. Then she showed him a video on her phone that explained how the wireless sound bar worked.

Our friend left the store excited and with new confidence. Soon the basement television room in his house was booming just like a movie theater.

Of course, the difference between Mike and Francine is clear: Francine was interested in the real job my friend wanted done. Instead of assuming she knew what our friend needed, she took responsibility for his needs and invested time to understand what "job" he was trying to do. The difference in outcomes was clear as well. Our friend went home thrilled after Francine explained everything to him.

COUNTERFEIT DISCOVERY

The counterfeit to discovering the real job to be done is to ask questions to sell or manipulate people rather than serve them and meet their true need. This sometimes happens if we solve the customer's problem from our own frame of reference, or if we rush to make a sale.

Picture someone who has been advised by her doctor to get more cardiovascular exercise so she can lose a few pounds and lower her cholesterol. She walks into a big sporting-goods store and says to the sales associate, "I'd like to buy a treadmill."

Well, one option for the sales associate is to point the customer toward the treadmills and say, "We have a great selection over there," which might be the lowest bar we set for customer care, right above ignoring the customer entirely. Beyond this meager response, though, there are three common counterfeits we see associates default to when responding to customer requests:

- Dazzle the customer.
- Provide false choices.
- Leave a false impression.

THE "DAZZLE THE CUSTOMER" COUNTERFEIT

"Treadmills? Sure! They're right over here. We just got this one in, the new CardioBlaster 9999, and we're offering it on sale. Great value! Look at this 60- by 20-inch belt. That 15 percent incline makes you work. There's a lifetime warranty on the motor and the frame, and it comes with a virtual-tour technology package we used to charge for, but now it's included. It's the best deal we've had in a long time."

This counterfeit response can be and usually is done with genuine excitement and interest, but it's excitement in the product rather than the customer. There's no empathy in connecting with or listening to the customer, and there's no responsibility for meeting the customer's real need. We do not know why she wants a treadmill. Actually, we don't know anything about her. However, we do know quite a lot about that amazing CardioBlaster 9999.

THE "PROVIDE FALSE CHOICES" COUNTERFEIT

Another way to approach the woman is to ask what she wants and then let her make a choice, all with the intent to make a sale. "What kind of treadmill were you looking for? We have a range of them, running from $429 to our top-of-the-line model at $2,000. Are you interested in a small one or a large one? How much are you looking to spend?"

OK, so now at least we're asking questions, which is a good thing. We're connecting, and perhaps trying to understand what features she'd like. The limitation in this counterfeit is that we're asking these questions from our frame of reference, and the questions won't get us very far in learning her hidden story or the real job to be done. We're still focused on the product instead of the need. Again, we're assuming the woman is looking for a *product*—the only remaining question is which one she should buy. In a sense, these are false choices. A treadmill would probably help the woman increase her cardiovascular health, but a treadmill is only one of many ways to do the job she wants done—and maybe not the best way for her.

THE "LEAVE A FALSE IMPRESSION" COUNTERFEIT

"You're looking for a treadmill so you can lower your cholesterol? This model here is a good option. Half-hour jogging on this model will lower your risk of a high-cholesterol diagnosis about 7 percent." The woman is impressed. This kid knows a lot about these machines. And yet, what he doesn't tell her is that a brisk half-hour walk in a $40 pair of shoes outdoors would also lower her "risk of a high-cholesterol diagnosis about 7 percent."

Whether he means to or not, the seller is leaving a false impression with the customer. What he's telling her is technically true—he's not lying—but he's giving her less than the full picture. Everybody knows about the pressure to sell, and especially to sell big-ticket stuff. Of course, he doesn't want to pass her off to the shoe department, since he's after the commission. But is he really taking responsibility for his customer by giving her such a tiny slice of truth?

By using these counterfeit responses, we miss the opportunity to discover the real job to be done and take responsibility for meeting the client's need.

WHY DON'T WE DISCOVER THE REAL JOB TO BE DONE?

In many cases, it's easy to assume we already know what the customer needs. We've heard the same question from dozens of customers before, so we just jump to the answer. We know our products so well that, of course, everyone needs this model right here. And sometimes we're right. But other times we are completely off, and we miss the opportunity to build loyalty. Shifting our paradigm from one of "having the answer" to "discovering the need" can make all the difference in our ability to earn loyalty.

A second reason why some associates aren't discovering the real job to be done is that they are being pressured to "make the sale" or "wrap up the call." We have targets to hit and benchmarks to meet. The excuse we hear is, "There simply isn't time." In situations like these, we have to get clarity on the organization's priorities and discover if *our real job to be done* is quicker call times, making the sale, or creating loyal customers. Meeting our customers' real needs must become our top priority if we want their loyalty.

HOW DO WE DISCOVER THE REAL JOB TO BE DONE?

Discovering the real job to be done begins with showing empathy and taking responsibility. We connect with our customers, listen, and learn why they came to us. Clayton Christensen says, "We all have many jobs to be done in our lives. Some are little (pass the time while waiting in line), some are big (find a more fulfilling career). When we buy a product, we essentially 'hire' it to help us do a job."[2] Discovering the real job to be done is as simple as knowing what our customer is "hiring" us to do.

You might remember our friend's terrible experience with Airline 1, trying to get to Boston for a meeting, and how the help-desk person at Airline 2 saved him. Airline 2 couldn't get him on a flight to arrive at his meeting in time, but the help-desk person did enable him to do the job he needed done: participate in the meeting in Boston. The Airline 2 employee owned his problem and resolved it. And that is very important to earning loyalty.

In order to discover the real job to be done, we need to do three things:

- Be curious, but not pushy.

- Ask for context.
- Lead with the need.

BE CURIOUS, BUT NOT PUSHY

Most customers don't want to be barraged with questions. A simple "I'm glad to help you; let me just make sure I understand what you need so that we don't spend time on the wrong solution" is a great way to begin the conversation without seeming pushy.

ASK FOR CONTEXT

A few simple, open-ended questions like "What are you hoping to accomplish?" or "What would you like this product or service to do for you?" or even "Why are you interested in this product or service?" will create a dialogue that quickly gets to the customer's job to be done.

Once you find out the job the woman really wants done—lose a few pounds and lower her cholesterol—what do you do then? It depends on what kind of person you are. This story told by a friend of ours will illustrate what we mean:

> I walked into the phone store to buy a new phone charger for my car. My old ones were acting weird—sometimes they charged up really fast and sometimes they didn't. I found a service person named Kes and asked if the store carried car chargers.
>
> "Sure, we have a bunch of those," he replied. "Step over here and I'll show you."
>
> The store was crazy busy, and I didn't really want to bother the guy for such a simple purchase, but he walked me over to the display and asked, "Why do you want a new phone charger?" Well, I thought that was an odd question ("Um, to charge my phone in the car?"), but I explained to him how frustrating it was dealing with the charging inconsistencies.
>
> Kes listened intently and then offered, "I'm not sure if you know this or not, but cars put out uneven voltage. The voltage can spike when you start the car or the A/C starts up. So your chargers might draw more or less power depending on the situation. Maybe you don't actually need a new one."
>
> I had never heard that before and suddenly it all made sense. Even though it was unlikely to change anything, I

> ended up buying a new charger anyway—I could always use a spare for when I traveled. After helping me at the register, Kes verified my contact information and offered me his card. "Here's my business card," he added with a smile. "I'll contact you in a couple of weeks to find out how it's working."
>
> And he did! I reported that my phone was still charging at different rates, but now I had the peace of mind of knowing *why*. And having used the new charger on a recent trip, I considered the whole experience to be a win-win in my book.
>
> Kes is no ordinary salesman. He's . . . different. He figured out what my real problem was and then he owned it.

The real problem, as it turns out, wasn't that our friend had a defective charger. The problem was he didn't know how his car's voltage worked. By taking the time to understand and address the real problem, Kes was rewarded with a sale anyway. And even if he hadn't been, Kes helped create another loyal customer. The "odd" question—"Why do you want a new phone charger?"—turned out to be the key to discovering the job to be done.

Increasingly, our jobs are to educate customers. More and more, we must be a consultant who takes on the responsibility of guiding, advising, and teaching. According to Debbie Hauss, who researches best practices in the retail business, "Whatever the product, the more information you provide to customers, the more likely they'll be to buy. It's human nature to appreciate help, information, and assistance in a store." Hauss wrote about the "great customer experience" she had shopping for hiking gear at an REI store:

> One REI associate in particular spent a lot of time talking through different hikes and trips we could take, sharing handbooks and maps that could guide our way. I might have been able to gather that information online, but his passion motivated me to purchase one of the books while in the store that day.[3]

Asking for context is particularly important in business-to-business (B2B) situations. As B2B sales expert Diane Gordon advises, "[Think] in terms of the customer's goals—what are they trying to do—vs. what our product does or what our service includes. Too often companies are all about the stuff they have versus what it can actually do to help the customer get their money's worth."[4]

LEAD WITH THE NEED

Once we've discovered the job to be done, it's time to lead with the need. Look at these two sentences. How are they different?

1. **"You'll want cushioned racing shoes."**

2. **"To do well in the upcoming marathon, you'll want cushioned racing shoes."**

The mentality behind Sentence 1 is, "I have a product to sell you."

The mentality behind Sentence 2 is, "You have a job to do, and this product will help you do that job."

Maybe it doesn't seem like much of a difference, but actually there's a huge gap between these two mentalities and what they convey to the customer. "Lead with the need" is simple—it means talking about the need before you talk about the product. A friend bought a new home high up on the side of a mountain in the western United States. In winter, he would have to move snow from his driveway, so he went to the store to buy a snowblower.

"Where do you live?" asked the grizzled salesman.

When our friend told him, the salesman clapped his hand on the biggest, most expensive machine in the store and said, "Then you'll need this model." It was a huge red monster that looked like one of those Zambonis they use to resurface an ice rink.

Our friend assumed the salesperson was trying to make a commission off of the sale and, with a skeptical chuckle, opted for a small, far less expensive model.

"OK," sighed the old gentleman, "but don't say I didn't warn you."

When the first winter storm hit with a fury, our friend found that his little 24-inch snowblower couldn't even move through the drifts piling up on his driveway. Our friend clearly didn't understand his own job to be done, and the salesman hadn't made much of an effort to educate him.

Now imagine if the same salesperson had decided to lead with the need: "You live above the 4,000-foot level. That means you're going to get several feet of snow every winter, which requires a lot of horsepower to move. That kind of heavy-duty snow removal calls for this 45-inch model."

Leading with the need means we keep the actual job to be done in our mental foreground. Too often the fatal tendency of even the most well-intentioned service people is to keep the *product* in the mental foreground. For example, a customer in the hardware department asks to buy a wrench; unless we find out what job they want the wrench to do, we really don't know if they need a wrench. But our reflex is to say, "The wrenches are right over there." At that point, we're not a service person, we're a GPS unit. Until we ask, we don't know if they want to fix a pipe or hit someone over the head with it. We don't know if they need an open wrench, a crescent wrench, a box wrench, a socket wrench, or a combination wrench.

CUSTOMER: Here's my problem. I'm trying to loosen the bolts on an old fence so I can remove it.

SALESPERSON: What do the bolts look like? Here are some sample bolts. Do they look like any of these?

CUSTOMER: They're just like this one with the straight edges.

SALESPERSON: That's a hex bolt. To remove hex bolts, you need a box wrench. It's designed to grab those edges on the head of the bolt. Here's a nice set of box wrenches.

This simple exchange shows that the customer-service person is responsible for the customer, understands the real job to be done, and is leading with the need.

Back to the earlier example of the woman who wanted to buy a treadmill. A responsible salesperson would want to know the reason behind the request—not to be nosy, but to find out the real job to be done.

WOMAN: I'd like to buy a treadmill.

SALESPERSON: Great, I'd be happy to help you with that. Can you tell me what you'd like to accomplish with your new treadmill?

WOMAN: I'm trying to lose a few pounds and lower my cholesterol.

SALESPERSON: Sounds good. Have you used treadmills in the past?

WOMAN: Well, only a few times at the gym. But my friend has one, and she swears by it. It seems to be working wonders for her.

SALESPERSON: Absolutely. Walking and running can both be great forms of exercise. Before we start exploring models, is there anything else that would help me get you matched up with the right treadmill?

WOMAN: I do have knee trouble, so I'm a little worried about the pain in my right knee.

SALESPERSON: Right. Running and walking can sometimes aggravate knee pain. We have a few machines that will be easier on your knees and that are still great options to increase your fitness level. Have you tried an elliptical machine at your gym?

Discovering the real job might sound simple, but it requires a lot of empathy and a strong sense of responsibility. Simply giving customers "what they ask for" may sound like good customer service, but it's only when we help customers solve their *real problem* that we're truly on the road to earning their loyalty.

LEADER APPLICATION—
THE PRACTICE OF DISCOVERING THE REAL JOB TO BE DONE

Beyond modeling this practice, it is critical for leaders to create an environment where discovering the real job to be done is not only tolerated but celebrated. If an employee goes over the average handle time in your call center but is meeting customers' real needs in the calls, recognize that employee for his or her efforts in building loyalty. If your sales associate punts the sale to another department because it's the right thing for the customer, celebrate that person's contribution to increasing customer loyalty.

Enabling your team members to fulfill the real needs of customers allows them to contribute to something beyond just filling orders or answering questions, and this is what gives their work meaning. Dr. Schon Beechler, a top scholar and researcher at the INSEAD School of Business, wrote:

> **When people feel that they are pursuing a profound purpose or engaging in work that is important personally, there are significant positive effects such as reductions in stress, turnover, absenteeism, dissatisfaction, cynicism, and depression. In addition, research shows increases in commitment, happiness, satisfaction, engagement, effort, and empowerment, and a sense of fulfillment among those who find meaning in their work.**[5]

There's nothing quite like the feeling of doing a job that really needs to be done—both for you and for team members.

HUDDLE 6—DISCOVER THE REAL JOB TO BE DONE

Search for the underlying need or goal.

1. **CELEBRATE**

   Celebrate someone who took responsibility for a customer's needs.

2. **LEARN**

   Discuss the following questions:

   a. When have you felt rushed or pushed by a salesperson?

   b. What kinds of "jobs" do customers want us to do for them?

   c. How is "listening to learn" different from "discovering the real job"?

   d. To find out the "real" Job to Be Done, what should we ask?

3. **COMMIT**

   Discover the "real" Job to Be Done for a customer.

4. **SCHEDULE FOLLOW-UP**

   Huddle 7 date/time? Who will lead?

CHAPTER 7

FOLLOW UP TO STRENGTHEN THE RELATIONSHIP

―――

"FOLLOW-UP OFFERS THE SATISFACTION OF A JOB WELL DONE WHEN THE COMMENTS ARE POSITIVE, AND COURSE CORRECTIONS WHEN THEY ARE NEGATIVE."
—FRED REICHHELD

The manager of a sporting-goods store, Curtis (remember him from Chapter 3?), is required to make follow-up phone calls to customers who give the store a low-satisfaction rating. He dislikes this part of his job and usually puts it off as long as he can. Eventually, though, he braces himself and gets on the phone with people he knows are unhappy with him. It's an ordeal. Let's listen in:

CURTIS: Ms. Sadek? I'm Curtis Lopez, manager at SportStuff store.

SADEK: What do you want?

CURTIS: On our customer-satisfaction survey, you rated us 3 out of 10. And you know, I find that surprising, because we're so committed to customer service. Why don't you tell me about the service you got on, uh, May 23.

SADEK: You people are a joke.

CURTIS: What do you mean, *a joke*?

SADEK: Your people were laughing at me through the whole transaction. Right in front of me.

CURTIS: I find it hard to believe that our SportStuff specialists would do that sort of thing.

SADEK: Specialists? That's a laugh. What do they specialize in? Making fun of your customers? If you're the manager, where were you, anyway? I was looking for you.

CURTIS: Well, that was my day off.

SADEK: You're the manager, and you're not even there.

CURTIS: Don't you ever get a day off, Ms. Sadek?

SADEK: You're just wasting my time.

CURTIS: OK, let's cut to the chase. What would it take to move you from a 3 to a 10?

SADEK: Goodbye!

Curtis has never been very good at this. Even so, this was an unusually bad follow-up call. He did just about everything wrong and turned disappointment into disgust. He became defensive and has no doubt lost any possibility of converting Ms. Sadek into a loyal customer.

WHAT DOES "FOLLOW UP TO STRENGTHEN THE RELATIONSHIP" LOOK LIKE?

Those who have engendered true loyalty effectively follow up with their customers. It goes with doing the "job to be done." How can we know if we actually did the job right unless we follow up to find out?

- Auto repair: "How is that new windshield on the truck working out for you?"

- Uniform-rental company: "How does your team like the new uniforms we delivered last week?"

- Remodeler: "Is there anything at all we can do to improve the paint job we did for you?"

- Photographer: "Did your kids like the new family portrait? If anyone's unhappy, we'll gladly do what we can to fix it."

- Insurance agent: "Are you happy with the way we handled your claim? What could we have done better?"

Our service might have been just fine, but that doesn't mean it stayed fine. And we can always improve. We should be asking the question, "What can we do better?" Unless we're constantly upgrading what we do, the loyalty of our customers may be at risk. Follow-up is not hard if we really mean to be helpful. We like the way marketing expert Rebecca Wilson put it:

> **If you follow up reluctantly, avoid it altogether, or lack sincerity when you do follow up, people can sense it and will treat you accordingly. Whereas, when you follow up consistently, with confidence, respect, and a keen, honest desire to build an ongoing relationship with your target, people can tell . . . and they are often appreciative.[1]**

As Rebecca Wilson pointed out, follow-up is more than just a courtesy. It's an opportunity to build the relationship, and that may be the best reason of all for doing consistent follow-up. If we see a customer interaction as a one-off event, that customer isn't likely to feel connected to us.

Ask yourself, which would you be loyal to: a provider who sees you as a number in a queue, or a provider who treats you with warmth and empathy, does the job you really need done, and follows up to make sure you're happy?

Many organizations now have whole systems for following up with customers. There are online surveys and paper surveys, text messages, robocalls, and calls from real humans—all asking us to rate their service. To customers, it feels like "relentless tugs on the sleeve," says the *New York Times*.

According to management professor Richard L. Oliver of Vanderbilt University, "The frequent requests to fill out these surveys, especially with no incentives, have been so annoying that people just stop doing it."[2]

Does this mean you shouldn't follow up with customers? Not at all. Follow-up doesn't require an elaborate survey system. And even if your company does it that way, you should still follow up on your own—for the good of your team and your personal relationship with the customer. You can ask customers quick questions like:

- "What could we have done better?"

- "What kind of help were you looking for?"

- "What else could we have done for you?"

Questions like these can provide timely information to share with your team. Informal, face-to-face follow-up is far more effective than, say, email surveys. In fact, research shows that personal requests for information are thirty-four times more likely than an email survey to get a useful response.[3]

We can get the equivalent of dozens of "completed surveys" each day simply by asking customers a question or two. Wouldn't you rather do that than wait to follow up after the customer has trashed you on Yelp, Google, or Facebook?

Beyond this informal kind of follow-up, some surveys can be quite useful. Ideally, the survey identifies unhappy customers to follow up with so we can understand concerns, fix problems, and prevent issues from happening again. We should also follow up with those who are lukewarm about their experience with us, as well as our happiest and strongest promoter customers. Every customer can teach us how to get better. Promoters, for example, often have great ideas, since they are invested in our success. Furthermore, learning *who* on our team is doing a great job for customers, then celebrating that employee's achievements, is one of the best ways to inspire our team and build loyalty.

COUNTERFEIT FOLLOW-UP

The opposite of following up is giving up, dropping the ball, walking away, or thinking "out of sight, out of mind." In doing these things, we're obviously not taking responsibility for building the customer relationship. Counterfeit follow-up is equally irresponsible, and it involves:

- Showing interest only to protect ourselves.

- Asking questions without caring about the response.

When checking out of a store, we sometimes hear, "Find everything you need?" from an employee whose head is down, isn't making eye contact, and quite frankly doesn't seem to care if we found everything or not. Customers can quickly spot rote and robotic routines like these. If loyalty is important to us, we can do better, even if it's only a friendly farewell. No follow-up is better than phony counterfeit follow-up. Taking a genuine interest in learning what we could have done better goes a long way toward earning another person's loyalty.

WHY AREN'T WE FOLLOWING UP TO STRENGTHEN THE RELATIONSHIP?

It takes time. "How," you might ask, "do I do genuine, personal follow-up and still take care of all the other demands on my time?" Of course, effective follow-up does take time, but in our opinion, it often takes a lot less time (and expense) to find out about a problem *now* and fix it, rather than wait, learn about it later, and have to sort it out then.

Dealing with conflict is challenging. Most customer-service training focuses on "recovery" from mishaps or "defusing" conflicts. "Defuse" is what bomb squads do. Your team members shouldn't have to defuse customer anger—at least, not very often—if they are practicing the loyalty principles and practices. But mistakes and misunderstandings do happen. That's why we provide you with a proven method for dealing with conflict—both with customers and coworkers—through the balance of this chapter.

HOW DO WE FOLLOW UP TO STRENGTHEN THE RELATIONSHIP?

In a conflict situation, customers want more than just a "defusing" of their feelings. They want the job done. That's where conscientious follow-up comes in. Let's rewind the story of Curtis and Ms. Sadek, the unhappy customer, and see how things would have gone if Curtis had followed up effectively with her.

CURTIS: Ms. Sadek? I'm Curtis Lopez, manager at SportStuff store.
SADEK: Yes?
CURTIS: I understand you had a real problem when you came into our store on Tuesday. We're always trying to serve our customers

better, and it would be so helpful if you could give me some input on your experience at the store.

SADEK: Well, OK. I bought this new pedometer to track my walking, but I couldn't figure out how it worked. The instructions were impossible to follow. So I came in for help. I stood around for several minutes waiting. No one acknowledged I was there. When they finally did help, they kept getting interrupted and seemed impatient, like they thought I wasn't "getting it" and just wanted to get rid of me.

CURTIS: Wow, Ms. Sadek, I'm really sorry to hear that. I can't imagine how difficult that would be. I want to apologize. That is unacceptable. We never want a customer to feel that way.

SADEK: I couldn't figure out how to sync it up with my computer, and your people seemed to be laughing at me.

CURTIS: Again, I apologize. I'd like to meet you and personally see that you get what you need. I'm happy to help. Would it be possible for you to come by again?

SADEK: I don't have a lot of time. I'm leaving on a walking tour the day after tomorrow. I wanted to get this thing set up first. But I have about an hour tomorrow afternoon, around four o'clock.

CURTIS: Ms. Sadek, I'd really like to get you set up before you leave. Could you come by at four o'clock tomorrow?

SADEK: Depends. How much will it cost?

CURTIS: Oh, it won't cost you anything for me to set up the pedometer and sync it to your computer.

SADEK: OK. Sounds like a great offer. Thanks.

CURTIS: Ms. Sadek, I'm so sorry about this problem. I look forward to seeing you tomorrow. We really value your business.

Now Curtis is well on the way toward earning Ms. Sadek's loyalty. Let's look closely at how he handled this follow-up call.

THE FIVE "A'S"

There are five "A's" to remember when doing follow-up, especially in a conflict situation. All five A's were present in *Responsible* Curtis's phone call with Ms. Sadek:

- *Assume* others have good intent.

- *Align* with the person's emotions.

- *Apologize* with your heart and without a hint of defensiveness.

- *Ask* how you can make things right.
- *Assure* the person you will follow through, then do it.

Let's unpack each of these as we compare the two calls to Ms. Sadek—the first one from *Irresponsible* Curtis, and the second one from *Responsible* Curtis.

ASSUME OTHERS HAVE GOOD INTENT

In the first interaction with Ms. Sadek, Irresponsible Curtis assumed she was just another cranky, hard-to-please customer. Responsible Curtis assumed the opposite—that she did not intend to be unfair. If we assume unhappy customers are trying to take advantage to get "freebies," we will come across with an attitude that puts them immediately on the defensive. Instead, we need to give our customers the benefit of the doubt, even if temporarily. In showing empathy, we'll hear them out and do our best to understand their point of view. Are there customers who will try to take advantage of us? Yes, but they are outliers. Most are not like that. In addition, don't assume your customers are trying to swindle you. We're not in favor of giving away the store, but a prompt offer of compensation for a foul-up is not only a good way to earn loyalty, but also a decent thing to do. Extending trust to people usually pays off in the long run.

ALIGN WITH THE PERSON'S EMOTIONS

By this, we mean align your response to the customer's emotions. We do not mean you should get angry if the customer is angry. "Alignment" means getting on the customer's side, even if temporarily.

As soon as Irresponsible Curtis heard "You people are a joke," he turned cranky. But after Responsible Curtis heard her story, he aligned with her by saying, "Wow, Ms. Sadek, I'm really sorry to hear that. I can't imagine how difficult that would be." Now he is on her side.

As we shared in our empathy discussion, we need to make the emotional connection first and then deal with the job to be done. Unhappy customers need to get "psychological air." Strong emotions are like suffocation: They've got to be able to breathe before they can move on to anything else. People who are suffocated by anger or frustration need, first of all, to be listened to—they need emotional oxygen. If they're upset, let them vent. Let them get it all out. Use your empathy skills to make a warm connection and listen to learn. Stand with them, not against them.

APOLOGIZE WITH YOUR HEART
AND WITHOUT A HINT OF DEFENSIVENESS

A heartfelt apology not only melts anger, but it is also the right thing to do when we're at fault. Even if we're not at fault, we can practice empathy by feeling "with" other people and expressing regret for a bad experience.

Tossing out a half-felt apology, a businesslike "Sorry about that" without much feeling in it, only makes matters worse. Note that Irresponsible Curtis never even tried to apologize, whereas Responsible Curtis apologized four times. Obviously, we should align to the customer's feelings, and sometimes a cheerful "sorry" is all they need from us. But in a conflict situation, we may need to apologize over and over until we are sure the customer really hears us and believes what we are saying.

Getting defensive, as Irresponsible Curtis did ("I find it hard to believe that our SportStuff specialists would do that sort of thing"), is a recipe for escalating conflict and never a good idea. We may feel a certain satisfaction when we win the fight and the other person loses, but we'll destroy loyalty in the process. As Seth Godin observes, you can always get the best of the argument, if that's important to you.

> In most interactions, you're capable of winning. If you push hard enough, kick someone in the shins, throw a tantrum, cheat a little bit, putting it all at stake, you might very well get your way. But often this sort of winning is actually losing. That's because we rarely have an interaction only once, and [our] reputation and connection are at stake.[4]

The defensive apology is a loyalty killer. Consider what happened one Sunday when an airline overbooked a flight and selected a passenger for deboarding. The airline had a legal right to remove him, but he didn't want to go, so he was dragged from the plane and injured in the process. Videos of the debacle popped up on the internet, raising a worldwide storm of protest.

The airline tweeted a statement from the chief executive apologizing for "having to re-accommodate" passengers but saying nothing about the man who was physically dragged from the plane and bloodied. Then, in another statement (also shared on Twitter), the CEO stated that the airline's employees had "followed established procedures for dealing with situations like this," and he described the passenger as "disruptive" and "belligerent." In response, Twitter users began trashing the airline while the storm of anger got worse. Marketing experts noted the CEO's response amounted to a classic non-apology, an empty statement that acknowledges an event, but shirks responsibility. The airline's shares plunged in value.

On Tuesday, the airline issued another statement from the CEO. To his credit, he said, "I deeply apologize to the customer forcibly removed and to all the customers aboard. No one should ever be mistreated this way. I want you to know that we take full responsibility and we will work to make it right. It's never too late to do the right thing." True enough; furthermore, it's never too *early* to do the right thing.

ASK HOW YOU CAN MAKE THINGS RIGHT

Where Irresponsible Curtis was only interested in improving his customer-satisfaction score ("What would it take to move you from a 3 to a 10?"), Responsible Curtis said: "I'd like to meet you and personally see that you get what you need. I'm happy to help." After finding out Ms. Sadek's job to be done, he laid out a course of action that would make things right for Ms. Sadek. He offered more help than she expected, a good practice for recovering from a mess-up. Maybe it's personal service. Maybe it's a free-rental day. Maybe you pick up the check. Whatever it is, offer it—the gesture might help win you the person's loyalty after all.

ASSURE THE PERSON YOU WILL FOLLOW THROUGH, THEN DO IT

There's no question that Responsible Curtis will follow through exactly. He specified the job he would do and when he would do it, and, as a result, the customer noticeably changed her attitude.

CLOSING THE LOOP

In addition to using the five A's to defuse a conflict and turn a potential detractor into a promoter, Fred Reichheld recommends "closing the loop" to find out what caused the problem in the first place and then do an appropriate fix.[5] Reflecting on the incident when the passenger was dragged from an airplane, the airline CEO confessed that the whole thing was a "system failure" and that the airline had not provided its managers and supervisors with "the proper tools, policies, and procedures that allow them to use their common sense. . . . That's on me. I have to fix that."

He was right. The CEO's job is to make sure we have a good system, but as customer-facing managers and employees, we're responsible for closing the loop, even if we don't have a good system. If something bad happens, ask yourself, *What are the root causes of this incident? What is the standard we should be meeting? Why aren't we meeting that standard? What could we do to prevent or at least reduce the chances of something like this happening again?* The answers to these questions often come from following up with customers to learn more details about the incident.

Sure, many customers don't care about the root causes of their problem, but we should so that we can prevent it from cropping up again. So we tell customers we are trying to improve the quality of our service, and their help will be valuable in pinpointing issues. If customers feel like we care about their opinion and appreciate their willingness to share it, we can turn them into partners in making our business better. And in doing so, their confidence in our ability to serve them better in the future will grow.

Sometimes we're asked: "Should we follow up further, after we have already addressed a problem, and if so, when?" This depends. In some circumstances we agree with customer-service expert John Mehrmann:

> When possible, follow up (again) with the customer after sufficient time has elapsed to demonstrate that the corrective action has been effective. A phone call or a personalized postcard demonstrates individual attention and acknowledgment. Demonstrating compassion and attentiveness thirty days after a problem has been resolved is a powerful message to show that you really do care about the individual customer. This follow-up after the anger has subsided and the corrective action has been demonstrated as effective may be enough to retain loyal customers and earn a few new ones.[6]

Imagine how Ms. Sadek would feel if Curtis called her thirty days later and asked how the pedometer worked on her walking tour. We will cover this kind of generous, unexpected behavior in Chapters 8 and 10.

Sometimes a customer's problem takes time to solve. So we need to own it all the way to the solution, no matter how long it takes. Our persistence alone might earn the loyalty of an unhappy customer.

What about online customers? Do they really care if we own their issues and follow up with them? Scholars in Germany studied this very question and concluded that follow-up is just as vital to remote customers as it is to face-to-face customers.[7] All of the guidelines we've talked about apply equally well to customers on the floor, online, or on the phone.

The best follow-up might come in two phases: one prompt, one delayed. Don't let the problem hang; on the other hand, don't solve and forget. Be quick and slow. Fix the hair in the soup immediately; then email/text/ring up the customer in a couple of weeks, apologize again, and offer a nice reward for coming back. Create reminders so you'll remember to follow up in the future.

However you do it, don't ignore the power of follow-up. You owe it to unhappy customers to rebuild their trust. As Mike Templeman, founder of Foxtail Marketing and a digital marketing expert, wrote, "What happens when a customer complains about some aspect of your brand, but doesn't get a response? More likely than not, they will transfer their dissatisfaction to conversations with friends, coworkers, and family, putting your company in a bad light as a result. As if that bad word of mouth wasn't enough, the effect multiplies on social media. After all, your dissatisfied customers have the perfect outlet to vent their frustrations with the world right at their fingertips. An angry customer resulting in his best friend perceiving your brand in a negative light is not good. That same angry customer negatively influencing the brand perceptions of hundreds of social-media connections and friends is infinitely worse."

LEADER APPLICATION—THE PRACTICE OF FOLLOWING UP TO STRENGTHEN THE RELATIONSHIP

If you are a manager, your team can't do effective follow-up unless you let them. We've all been in a situation where someone couldn't solve our problem because they weren't allowed to, and it's as frustrating for the employee as it is for us. As a loyalty leader, you want a team of people who can take responsibility and solve problems by themselves. Micah Solomon said, "Hire for conscientiousness: detail orientation, including an ability and willingness to follow through to completion."[8] But no matter the makeup of your team, if you're consistent about it, you can teach the follow-up guidelines. It's a vital part of your job.

When you make follow-up phone calls, invite team members to listen in. Ask them to shadow you when you do a quick, in-person follow-up with customers. Let them critique you. When there's a mishap, let your team members see you practice the guidelines: assume good intent, get on the customer's side, offer a heartfelt apology, make things right, and follow through on your commitments. Don't toss blame around. Getting on the customer's side does not mean ganging up on a team member. If a team member makes a mistake, correct it in private.

Practice the same follow-up guidelines with team members. Assume that your team members have good intent, even when there's a problem. Certainly they don't come to work planning to mess up. Align with their emotions, even if temporarily—make sure they know that you understand their feelings. Above all, follow through on any commitments you make to one another. Don't leave things hanging. In Chapter 9, we'll cover how to share insights with team members in a way that earns their loyalty.

HUDDLE 7—FOLLOW UP TO STRENGTHEN THE RELATIONSHIP

Follow up to learn if the need was met, what you could have done better, and resolve concerns.

1. **CELEBRATE**

   Celebrate someone who discovered the "real" Job to Be Done for a customer.

2. **LEARN**

   Discuss the following questions:

   a. What problems do customers have? How can we prevent them?

   b. Which of the five A's do we need to improve on?

   c. What's the difference between a fake and a heartfelt apology?

   d. What are examples of "making it right" for customers?

3. **COMMIT**

   Follow up with a customer to learn how to get better.

4. **SCHEDULE FOLLOW-UP**

   Huddle 8 date/time? Who will lead?

PART
FOUR

THE PRINCIPLE
OF GENEROSITY

CHAPTER 8

THE NEED FOR GENEROSITY

"YOU GIVE BUT LITTLE WHEN YOU GIVE
OF YOUR POSSESSIONS. IT IS WHEN YOU
GIVE OF YOURSELF THAT YOU TRULY GIVE."
—KAHLIL GIBRAN

Generosity, the third of the Three Core Loyalty Principles, is straightforward. Generous people are kind. They extend themselves to help others. They think of new, creative things they can do for customers and coworkers. They may not save pennies in the short term, but they earn big dollars in the long term. More than that, they love people and treat them like guests. A friend shared this experience with us:

> One day at lunchtime, I went into a fast-food restaurant to get a burger. It was a nice place with clean tables, attractive blue-and-white paint on the walls, and cheerful helpers. My lunch cost $7.88, and I gave the attendant a $10 bill. Instead of making exact change for me, the young man handed me a $5 bill.
>
> "Um, this is $5," I said. "You only owe me $2.12."
>
> "Yes, sir, but I've run out of $1 bills, so I've given you the next largest bill I have."
>
> "But why?"
>
> "That's our policy, sir. Enjoy your lunch."
>
> As I sat enjoying my lunch, I thought about the kind of thinking that must have gone into that policy. What could have motivated the management to opt for such a thing? They could lose money every time a cashier faces that situation, and it must wreak havoc with their accounting. Something else must outweigh those concerns. To make exact change in that situation, the cashier might have to go somewhere else and get some bills, perhaps from a fellow cashier or from the manager's safe. That would take time. The customer would have to wait for change. Apparently, they value their customers' time more than the money they may lose on a particular transaction.
>
> As I got up to leave, an attendant handed me a free soft drink for the road. I'd never seen that before either. Apparently, this restaurant likes to give customers more value than they expect in lots of generous little ways. Do I go back there for lunch? You bet I do—as often as I can. I am a very loyal customer.

This restaurant doesn't have big discount days or a loyalty program. They simply treat people generously—just as we treat guests in our home. A person with a generous mindset acts differently from other people when a problem arises. Ask yourself, *How generous is our mindset?* Then think about your own business.

- **Retail:** When we see a customer walk into the store with a bag and a receipt in hand, what are our thoughts? How would a generous person react?

- **Software support:** A frantic user calls with a problem and an urgent deadline, but it's not immediately clear if the problem is with our software or their computer. How would a generous person handle this?

- **Healthcare:** An impatient patient wants to see her doctor *now*. We know it's not going to happen, so what do we do?

- **Government:** An angry citizen calls to complain about user fees. What is our immediate reaction? How would a generous person act in this situation?

- **Hospitality:** A guest with a shaky voice demands to speak to our manager. What instincts and reflexes take over? How would a generous person respond?

Generous people and organizations show kindness first, then they do whatever possible to give more than is expected. Zappos helps customers find shoes they don't have in stock. The famous Danish candy maker Anthon Berg gave a complimentary chocolate to every customer. Dick's Sporting Goods accepts expired coupons. These are just ordinary courtesies, but we have learned over many years and with lots of experience that ordinary generosity can be extraordinary—and it can earn real loyalty.

WHAT DOES GENEROSITY LOOK LIKE?

It was a routine call for the firefighters of Station 4 in Baytown, Texas. John McCormick had collapsed while mowing his lawn. The sixty-five-year-old man had a history of heart trouble, but the emergency crew was able to revive him and, according to procedure, followed him to the hospital.

But afterward, they didn't return to the fire station. Instead, they went back to John McCormick's home and finished mowing his lawn—backyard and front yard—cleaned everything up, and locked the mower away in the garage. Before they left, they posted a letter to Mrs. McCormick on her front door:

> **We felt bad that your husband didn't get to finish the yard, so we did.**
>
> **We are very sorry that your husband became ill, and we hope he has a speedy recovery.**
>
> **Let us know if there is anything we can do to help you out.**
> **Baytown Fire Department, Station 4, A-Shift**

Unknown to the team, a neighbor made a video of their kind deed and posted it on the Facebook page of the city of Baytown. The story went viral, and the firefighter team was deluged with thanks and congratulations, with notes from as far away as New Zealand.

"It wasn't that big of a deal just to help someone out at the worst time of their life," one of the team members said. But with that simple act of kindness, the firefighters of Baytown Station 4 showed the world what generosity looked like. Often it takes just a few more steps.

- What was the incentive for these firefighters to do what they did?

- Were they looking for repeat business?

- Were they angling for better customer-satisfaction scores?

Of course not. The impulse to help their fellow human beings arose from their hearts, not from some strategy to increase customer loyalty. Did they need permission to treat the man that way? Possibly. Sometime, somehow, their leader had given the OK to this team to behave generously toward the people of Baytown. Mowing a sick neighbor's lawn is not in their job description, but there must be something in the culture of that fire department that encourages this sort of generous response to a need.

Are you and the people on your team driven more by job descriptions, policies, and systems, or by the urge to enrich lives and give of yourselves?

Sometimes the dogged search for efficiency can come at the expense of generosity. For example, consider the list of the top ten things customers rate as "tremendously annoying," according to Consumers Union[1]:

1. **Can't get a human on the phone.**

2. **Salesperson is rude.**

3. **Many phone steps needed.**

4. **Long wait on hold.**

5. **Unhelpful solution.**

6. **Salesperson is too pushy.**

7. **Extras are pitched.**

8. **No apology for unsolved problem.**

9. **Can't find store salesperson.**

10. **Boring hold music or messages.**

Note how many of these items are about wasting the customer's time—nearly all of them. A basic principle of generosity is sensitivity to hassles and time-wasters. Most of these ungenerous behaviors are caused by organizational policies or systems. In pursuit of efficiency, some organizations end up annoying their customers by making them wait for service.

Imagine you have been invited to a neighbor's home for a dinner party. You ring the bell. No one answers, but tinny music plays over an intercom while a recorded voice tells you how important you are and that someone will be with you shortly. This goes on for ten minutes or so until your neighbor deigns to let you in. At that point, he abruptly asks you to wait in the entryway while he deals with another dinner guest for another fifteen minutes. Then he unaccountably disappears. You go looking for him. . . .

Thousands of customers live through a version of this absurd scenario each day. But some customers are so used to it, they bear their annoyance patiently until it gets out of hand. Then they react as any ill-treated human being would: They get mad, they make loud comments, they walk out. Even if they stay and suffer in silence, they certainly don't look upon us with fond loyalty.

That's why we were so impressed with the burger restaurant that didn't make our friend wait even a few seconds for change. It was a small gesture, but it showed that management was thinking hard about ways to spare his time and effort. Be generous with your own time, but not with the customer's. Anything you can do to save the customer time and effort will be perceived as generous. That's why:

- Zappos delivers orders before they say they will.

- Burt Brothers Tire & Service regularly finishes the work on your car early.

- Enterprise reps use handheld devices to check out customers returning cars instead of forcing them to stand in line at a cashier window.

Exceptional needs call for exceptional generosity. A customer in trouble will never forget you if you go out of your way to be generous. Leena tells about this experience:

> I often buy household items from a large online retailer.
> Once, I was waiting for a package containing many items
> with a total value of about $100. After waiting for a couple of
> days, I tracked the package and found—to my dismay—that
> it had already been delivered, and I had to assume it had
> been stolen from my front porch.
>
> I called the retailer to ask them to help me reorder all
> of the many items, hoping they had my information in their
> system, thus saving me time in the process. The customer-
> service representative on the phone listened and conveyed
> sympathy at my experience. After submitting the order, she
> explained that there would be no cost to replace the items,
> and she would be sending them overnight so that I wouldn't
> have to wait for them any longer.
>
> Talk about exceeding expectations! The retailer had
> already met their obligation: They had fulfilled my order
> and delivered the goods. It was completely outside of
> their responsibility to do any more. Yet, they were not
> only empathic, which made me feel better in a distressing
> situation, but they were also exceedingly generous in
> replacing the items at no cost. Years later, I've told the story
> dozens of times and am still a loyal customer.

Now, generosity is not all about giving away freebies; it's just as much about giving the customer some relief. For most of us, life is busy, hectic, and often highly stressful. What can we do to reduce rather than add to the customer's stress levels?

Most of us don't wake up each morning wondering how we can be more generous. But if we want loyal customers, that's what we should do. The opposite question should also be on our mind: What gets in the way of us being generous? Probably the biggest barrier to generosity is fear. Being generous can be risky. Customers might want more of our time and resources than we can give and still stay in business. Team members might demand more than their con-tribution justifies. Many of us live with accountants who examine our financial results constantly. It's tempting to play it safe and say "no" to anything that might trouble the delicate balance on that spreadsheet.

But it's been our experience that customers rarely demand more than you can reasonably give. They don't usually expect you to go to great lengths for them. In fact, a generous act can be as simple as opening a door, answering the phone on the first ring, or, as in the burger restaurant, cutting back on the hassle of making change.

UNGENEROUS (OR SCARCITY) THINKING

Two days before Valentine's Day, our friend dropped by a local bakery to buy some cookies for a family party. The heart-shaped frosted sugar cookies had been popular with his kids. He was pleased to find a dozen or so of them on display and asked the attendant to wrap them all up so he could take them home.

To his surprise, the man refused to sell him the cookies. "That will wipe me out. I won't have any more to sell," the attendant protested.

Our friend didn't know what to say to this. At last he countered, "Are you in the business of collecting cookies or selling cookies?" The attendant was undeterred, however, and refused to make the sale. Our friend left the bakery infuriated. To this day he's never returned.

The bakery attendant had a scarcity mindset, which is the opposite of a generous mindset. Scarcity makes people myopic, according to psychologist Shahram Heshmat. Myopia, of course, is nearsightedness. All you can see is *now*. "If you buy all my cookies, I won't have any left." The idea of making more cookies and thus more money seemed lost on the bakery attendant. He was, as Dr. Heshmat says, "exhibiting bias toward the here and now." There is no tomorrow, there is no enduring relationship with the customer, there is only this moment.

The scarcity mindset is a problem especially for someone behind a counter who might be young, inexperienced, untrained, and struggling just to get through the day. He might also be financially strapped, which means scarcity is a fearsome reality for him. He fears making mistakes; he fears violating policies he understands only partly.

For most of us, however, our first impulse is to be generous. According to psychologists, "generosity is the intuitive human response."[2] This explains why people are so willing to jump in and help someone in need. We make selfish decisions only when we have time to reason through them.

In an organization, where does the scarcity mindset come from? To a great degree it derives from management behavior. If the manager makes things like praise, recognition, rewards, training, communication, input, and feedback scarce, then fear and selfishness rule as the team members jockey for what few crumbs are available to them.

But if the manager is kind and generous with her time, praise, wisdom, and input, the mindset of the team will trend toward generosity. In the end, generosity is a character issue—a mindset of abundance rather than scarcity. Stephen R. Covey explained the difference between these two mindsets:

> **Most people are deeply scripted in what I call the Scarcity Mentality. They see life as having only so much, as though there were only one pie out there. And if someone were to get a big piece of the pie, it would mean less for everybody else. . . . The Abundance Mentality, on the other hand, flows out of a deep inner sense of personal worth and security. It is the paradigm that there is plenty out there and enough to spare for everybody. It results in sharing of prestige, of recognition, of profits, of decision making. It opens possibilities, options, alternatives, and creativity.[3]**

Generous people believe you can always bake more pie (or cookies). There is no limit to the pie. Generous people create opportunities so everyone can have as much pie as they want. Generous people are always thinking of what could be done for customers that's never been done before. They look past policies and systems to do what's best for customers. The CEO of an acclaimed financial institution in the midwestern United States has this philosophy:

> **No employee will ever get in trouble for doing what is right for the member. . . . There is only one operating policy or guideline you ever need. Trust your feelings. If it feels right and makes sense, do it on behalf of a member. Do not consider the system capability, policy, or procedure—err on doing whatever is necessary for the member and allow your manager to take care of the rest.[4]**

This philosophy of generosity has paid off for this leader, as the institution he leads has prospered way beyond expectations—an effect that business researcher Fred Kiel calls "the return on character." The manager's job in that company is to teach the team to be generous and then to "take care of the rest."

Any of the practices in this book, when overdone, can backfire and work to erode loyalty. Generosity is no exception, as Sandy experienced firsthand:

> **One day a renter showed up at one of our car-rental branches. The rep noticed that the man's driver's license had expired, so he couldn't legally rent the car. Our rep generously took the customer to the DMV to renew his license. That was great for this customer, but terrible for the ten other customers who came into the branch while our employee was at the DMV. It led to a coaching conversation with him about "balance."**

So we shouldn't be dumb about it. Nevertheless, the general rule should always be to do what's right for the customer. The CEO of a major toy retailer told us how disappointed he was about an incident in one of his stores. A young couple had bought clothing and toys for the baby they were expecting, but then they lost the baby. Devastated, the wife asked her husband to return the purchases. The husband took them back and told the store rep about their loss.

"I'm sorry to have to return these things. Maybe someday we'll come back."

"Gosh, I'm sorry," said the salesperson, "but you can't return things without receipts."

Well, the nasty letters flew. The company paid an awful price on social media. The CEO wrote a personal letter to the couple, apologized profusely, and tried his best to make it up to them. But the damage was done, and the company learned that some rules are primary (like treating people with generosity and empathy) and others are secondary (like requiring a receipt with a returned purchase).

This is a principle that is lost on many companies, and especially large ones. In the case of the airline that abused a customer, secondary rules got in the way of the primary rule of generosity, as Bill Taylor, editor of *Fast Company*, observed:

> **The problem wasn't with the airline's employees, but with a "rules-based culture" in which 85,000 people are "reluctant to make choices" that are not in the "tomes of rule books" and "giant manuals" that govern life at the airline. In**

> other words, employees at every level did what they were supposed to do—they followed the rules—yet the result was a total failure.[5]

We can see you throwing up your hands: "So am I supposed to follow company rules or not?" Our advice to you is the same as the advice Danny Meyer, legendary New York restaurateur and author of *Setting the Table*, gave to his team: "Err on the side of generosity. Apologize and make sure the value of the redemption is worth more than the cost of the initial mistake."[6] If you want loyal customers, generosity comes first—everything else is secondary.

Even when something bad happens, if you respond generously, the customer is even more likely to stay loyal to you. Marriott did a study of their own customers and divided them into three groups:

A = Nothing bad happened during the stay.

B = Something bad happened, but Marriott fixed the problem.

C = Something bad happened, but Marriott did not fix the problem.

They asked each of these groups if they would return to stay at a Marriott property. The response was surprising:

A = 89%

B = 94%

C = 69%

So customers who get their problems fixed turned out to be more loyal than customers who have never had a problem in the first place![7] Customer problems are great opportunities to show empathy, take responsibility, and be generous.

Sometimes you can't avoid a problem. You have to enforce a policy. You can't deliver because something failed up the chain. "Be generous with customers when you absolutely must break your service promise to them," says marketing scholar Leonard Berry. "Any compensation for a company's mistake should be unequivocally fair. Generosity is a trust builder; stinginess is a trust breaker."[8]

In Danny Meyer's words, "Generosity of spirit and a gracious approach to problem solving are, with few exceptions, the most effective way I know to earn lasting goodwill for your business."[9] Meyer also says that the value of generosity, kindness, and hospitality is "the degree to which it makes you feel good to make other people feel good."

There's plenty of science behind Meyer's observation. Neuroscientist Dr. Richard J. Davidson found that generosity, expressed as empathy, altruism, and other pro-social behaviors, reliably increased well-being, health, and even life expectancy.[10] Further research shows that generosity not only strengthens relationships, but also makes work more meaningful:

> **From a relationship perspective, givers build deeper and broader connections. When a salesperson truly cares about you, trust forms, and you're more likely to buy, come back for repeat business, and refer new customers. From a motivation perspective, helping others enriches the meaning and purpose of our own lives, showing us that our contributions matter and energizing us to work harder, longer, and smarter.[11]**

On the other hand, stinginess produces cortisol, the stress hormone. Researchers discovered that people who have difficulty sharing their resources begin to feel shame. The more miserly they behave toward others, the more shame and stress they experience.[12]

Generous employees are more likely to help one another, commit more to their work, and stay longer with the job. "More and more research illustrates the power of altruism," says Professor Donald Moynihan of the University of Wisconsin-Madison. "Helping others makes us happier. Altruism is not a form of martyrdom, but operates for many as part of a healthy psychological reward system."[13]

In summary, a generous person earns the loyalty and love of others. Generosity transforms customers and team members into advocates. How many advocates could your business use? But even more than this, generosity makes you feel better about yourself and your work.

LEADER APPLICATION— THE PRINCIPLE OF GENEROSITY

The Three Core Loyalty Principles for earning loyalty are empathy, responsibility, and generosity. Empathy enables us to understand another's feelings, responsibility is about owning that person's problem, and generosity means we go back and mow the sick man's lawn for him. You can create a generous team of people through your leadership, and if you hire new team members, you can hire people who are naturally generous.

LEADING YOUR TEAM

Generous leaders give the best they can to the team—sensitive input, loving feedback, training, encouragement, little surprises. Generosity doesn't always mean handing out goodies. A bonus might be nice now and then, but what team members really want is to feel that their ideas and their contributions are valued. Business author Erika Andersen, founding partner of Proteus and best-selling author, noted: "When an employee feels out of the loop, this can affect morale and confidence a great deal, as much or more so than material generosity can. At the worst, it makes a person feel unimportant."

That's why openly sharing information is so important to the team. Generous communication makes team members feel a part of the business and motivates them to help. Andersen also observes that teams are more loyal to a leader "who is generous with information, power, and well-deserved compliments." If we focus on practicing this third principle of loyalty, it becomes a habit and more natural to us.

Here are a few tips that can help:

Ask yourself, "Am I a generous person?" Decide what kind of person you want to be. Do you have a mindset of abundance or of scarcity? Do you feel comfortable sharing credit for success, or do you take the credit yourself? Are you open to ideas from the team, or does it have to be your idea to be any good? Do you tend to be kind and thoughtful, or callous and abrupt? Do you have a big heart or a pinched, stingy little heart? "Generous leaders view the world through a lens of abundance where much is to be gained rather than lost," says business thinker Margot Andersen. "This does not mean that they act in a 'fairy godmother' manner, granting wishes to all who ask. Rather, they place great value in genuinely connecting with their team."[14]

Look for "relief" opportunities. Question the entire process your customers go through. The writer Adam Gopnik observed, "People make rational decisions to invest in what they like and what gives them pleasure; the mistake is thinking of the product and not the entire social process."[15] Where can you make things easier for the customer and the team member? At what points can you simplify the customer experience? Where are you forcing them to wait? What might be annoying or confusing for them? Do you provide relief for the stresses of life, or do you add to them?

A powerful way to earn loyalty is to make it easy for customers to do business with you. "Effort should be reduced throughout the customer life cycle," says the Corporate Executive Board. "Our research demonstrates that reducing customer effort in pre- and post-sales customer touchpoints has measurable loyalty impact."[16]

Err on the side of generosity. Customer-facing employees make decisions every day about whether to give customers the benefit of the doubt. A customer might ask to return a product when it's not your policy to accept returns. A customer might dispute a bill. A customer might snap at you after waiting a long time for assistance. It might not seem fair to you, but if loyalty is what you're after, you're not going to demand absolute fairness. A thoughtful gesture is sometimes better than fairness. Enable your employees to do the right thing for customers.

Some customers might appear to be manipulative or mean, but it isn't very likely. We often make what's called the "fundamental attribution error," assuming that people act out of bad motives. When a customer shows impatience or annoyance, it's not usually because he's a jerk but because something in the situation moves him to act that way. Just because he's upset with you doesn't mean he's unkind to animals or not loved by his grandchildren. So give him a little extra loving care and look for ways to eliminate the annoyance, whatever it is.

HIRING NEW TEAM MEMBERS

Some people are naturally gifted with generosity. Researcher Helen Fisher has found that generosity is associated with one of the four basic temperament types linked to specific genes and hormonal patterns. She calls generous people "pioneers" because they keep the big picture in mind and are creative and imaginative, leading with surprising insights and ideas for engaging customers. They are also driven to make social attachments.[17]

A good way to recruit people who are naturally generous is to evaluate them in group interviews. At JetBlue Airways, for example, recruiters "watch how applicants interact with one another." This enables them to "assess communication and people skills to an extent that wouldn't be possible in a one-on-one setting."[18] For example, with a group of prospective employees, go around and ask each person to tell a story about something funny or embarrassing that happened to them. Then watch how the other candidates respond. Are they engaged with the speaker, or self-absorbed with thinking about what they are going to say? Evaluate facial expressions and body language to get a sense of their natural generosity to other people.

TWO PRACTICES OF GENEROUS PEOPLE

The key practices of generous people can be reduced to these:

- Share insights openly.
- Surprise with unexpected extras.

Because these two practices are fundamental to generosity, we'll study them in depth in the next two chapters. For now, let's ask ourselves how we extend generosity to our customers and to our team members. Do we look for opportunities to show kindness? To save them time and trouble? To surprise them with new and exciting experiences?

HUDDLE 8—
THE NEED FOR GENEROSITY

Generosity is giving from the heart more than is necessary or expected.

1. **CELEBRATE**

   Celebrate someone who followed up to learn from a customer.

2. **LEARN**

   Discuss the following questions:

   a. Who was generous to you? How did it feel?

   b. What difference does being generous make?

   c. What are the risks of being too generous?

   d. What gets in the way of being generous?

3. **COMMIT**

   Be generous to a customer or team member.

4. **SCHEDULE FOLLOW-UP**

   Huddle 9 date/time? Who will lead?

CHAPTER 9

SHARE INSIGHTS OPENLY

"LEADERSHIP IS THE ART OF GIVING PEOPLE A PLAT-
FORM FOR SPREADING IDEAS THAT WORK."
—SETH GODIN

MODEL . TEACH . REINFORCE

We're entering an era when more and more service jobs will be done by machines. It's coming on fast. Our purchases will arrive by drone; our food will be transported in driverless trucks; our consumer interactions will be overtaken by chatbots. Today nearly everything has an aspect of self-service built into it. And as this trend continues, there will be an increasing need to deliver the kind of value a machine can't—the kind of value at the heart of the humanistic principles of empathy, personal responsibility, and, above all, generosity. Embracing the principle of generosity means constantly thinking about new ways to make life easier and better for others by contributing thoughts, feelings, knowledge, and innovative ideas. The necessity of this contribution is why we express the key behavior as *share insights openly*. But to do so without the governing principle of generosity relegates this practice to complaints, criticism, and, in the ever-expanding world of self-service automation, indifference.

WHAT DOES IT LOOK LIKE TO SHARE INSIGHTS OPENLY?

Remember in Chapter 3, the sales associate in a red vest not only took time to teach Yasir how to tie his new tie, but also shared pointers with him on how to approach his job interview. In Chapter 6, Francine from the big electronics store generously took time to share with our friend how to install the transmitter on his television set so that his Bluetooth speaker worked. Then she showed him a video on her phone that explained how the wireless sound bar worked. Kes shared his knowledge about how car batteries put out uneven voltage, and that's why it may appear that our phone charger is not working at times. In each of these examples, the employees shared their knowledge and insights openly.

We have worked with several automotive-service chains over the years that provide everything from auto parts to oil changes to tires and brake jobs. One of the most effective ways we have seen them earn loyalty is to share information with customers about what their vehicle may need in the future, but only recommend a shorter list of things that really need to be addressed that day. "You may need to replace the rear tires in six months, but if it were my car, I would only worry about the front tires now." Educating customers and postponing a potential sale to a later date earns trust and is perceived as generous.

Sharing *our* insights to help customers can certainly earn their loyalty. And so does asking customers to share *their* insights with us— as described in Chapter 7, when we follow up and ask how we could have served them better. It feels good when others ask for our opinion and ideas because we all want to be useful, be valued, and make a contribution.

The same is true with our coworkers. We earn their loyalty both through sharing information to help them improve, and also from asking for their insights to help us improve. In this chapter, we concentrate on information sharing as an aspect of coaching to help other people get better. In Chapter 10, we address the loyalty-building impact of inviting our colleagues to share their ideas to help our team get better.

COUNTERFEIT SHARING

This is sharing without intending to help or make things better. Complaining, confronting, criticizing, or just plain gossiping about other people is not the kind of sharing we think about when trying to build true loyalty.

Criticism and gossip can be particularly damaging in a team environment. While gossiping builds social bonds, these bonds are often shallow and fragile. For those being gossiped about, the damage is obvious, as their reputation is essentially stolen from them. For those doing the gossiping, there is also a price to pay. Gossips erode personal credibility because it reflects insecurity and powerlessness, and also erodes their own trustworthiness and credibility.

WHY AREN'T WE SHARING INSIGHTS OPENLY?

We all have ideas and insights that can help others. Why do we sometimes hesitate to share them? One reason could be that we are busy and already have too much on our plate. Or perhaps we don't believe others will listen to us or care about what we have to say. More often, however, the reason we may not share our thoughts to help other team members is because we don't want to offend them or rock the boat. We can see their problems clearly, but choose to avoid potential conflict. Perhaps we lack confidence in our ability to share our insights in a way that will build a team member up. Our intention is clearly to help, not to hurt his or her feelings or undermine our relationship in any way.

HOW DO WE SHARE INSIGHTS OPENLY?

In addition to our loyalty huddles, where we regularly share ideas for creating more customer promoters (which we cover in detail in Chapter 10), we also need a team culture where it is not only safe, but people are encouraged to give what Fred Reichheld calls "loving feedback" to one another—very simply, sharing thoughts, feedback, and ideas with another person in a way that earns loyalty.

Think about a coach you may have had as part of an athletic team, a music ensemble, in an academic environment, or at work. There's nothing better than a great coach who has our best interests in mind, inspires us to get better, and helps us win. On our journey to increasing customer loyalty, all of us can use coaching—especially on the loyalty principles and practices. And coaching shouldn't just come from a manager to an employee. We need employees coaching each other and coaching their manager as well. In fact, many of the principles and practices throughout this book are part of the best practices coaches use with their colleagues and teams. While it is not the purpose of this book to create a framework specific to coaching, we'll touch on where coaching best practices intersect with the principles and key behaviors of loyalty. In this case, before we share our thoughts on how to provide "loving feedback" within a loyalty context, we'll look at an example of how *not* to coach:

CURTIS: Sue, I've got to talk to you. Listen, your attitude is unacceptable. I was on the phone with a customer just now, a Ms. Sadek, and I got an earful. You made her feel, well, honestly, talking about how dumb she is right in front of her? I tell you, she went off on *me.*

SUE: I didn't do that. She was returning a pedometer. She wanted her money back, and you know we can't—

CURTIS: (interrupting) Listen, your attitude isn't right. We're trying to create customer loyalty around here—

SUE: (interrupting) But I couldn't do what she wanted me to do. . . .

CURTIS: (obviously not listening) I've told you and told you, you need to *listen* to people with *empathy.* If you can't do that—

SUE: (interrupting) It was super busy. I didn't have time to—

CURTIS: (interrupting again) Why didn't you train her on the product? If she'd had training, she wouldn't have had the problem. I gotta go, Sue. Go back and reread how to treat customers with *empathy.* I'm going to have to put a note in your file.

Although this is a tongue-in-cheek example, we can learn a few things from it. First, a good coach is, above all, a good model. Unempathic-Irresponsible-Ungenerous Curtis is doing his best to show Sue how *not* to show empathy.

Second, a good coach is a two-way communicator, but Curtis is communicating only one way. There's no generosity in that. We often think of coaching as "telling," but it needs to be just as much about our Chapter 4 skill, listening to learn. By the way, the opposite is just as bad: giving no direction at all, expecting employees to solve problems without coaching from us. This is *abdicating* the responsibility we discussed in Chapter 5 that is needed to earn true loyalty. Some managers say, "Don't just come to me with a problem, tell me how you're going to solve it." *Well, OK, then I won't talk with you about problems I can't figure out on my own. And if I can figure it out on my own, why would I need to talk with you?*

Finally, a coach looking to build loyalty doesn't command people to change their ways. Communication expert Joseph Grenny said: "When people are told they need to change a habit, the typical response is to rebel. . . . The trick is not to lecture your employees. . . . Instead, ask questions—treat the coaching session like an interview. Help them uncover motivations they already have."[1]

Now let's observe Empathic-Responsible-Generous Curtis taking a different approach in coaching Sue:

CURTIS: Sue, I really appreciate the job you've been doing the last few days, even though it's been crazy. I just wanted to clear something up. What do you remember about a Ms. Sadek who tried to return a pedometer? I really want to hear your perspective.

SUE: Well, she brought the pedometer back and said, "I can't make heads or tails out of this thing and I want my money back." She was really ticked off. So, what I said was, "Can I help you figure it out?" But she was *on* one. What she really wanted was a refund, and you know we can't do that. Besides, we were super busy that day.

CURTIS: It's tough on days like that. The part that concerned me—and that I know would concern you—is that the customer felt like you were impatient with her or making fun of her. Do you know why she could have felt that way?

SUE: I guess she felt dumb because she couldn't get it to work on her own. It's frustrating for us because some customers need a lot more help than others.

CURTIS: You're not alone—it *is* frustrating. What about this idea? There's some empathic language you can use with this kind of customer. I can walk you through it. Can we talk for about ten minutes tomorrow at nine? How does that sound?

SUE: Yeah, I'd like to know how to handle these people. I get one or two every day, and they hold everything up.

This time, Curtis shows empathy by listening to Sue and acknowledging her feelings. He takes responsibility for helping her. And he shows generosity by recognizing that Sue has good intentions and that her side of the story is just as much worth considering as the customer's. Curtis is now coaching Sue in a way that will help increase her loyalty to the team and will also increase their customers' loyalty to the store—a tricky balance to achieve.

Coaching that builds loyalty is a sharing of insights. A great insight isn't worth much if we can't share it effectively and get others to act on it. Here are some loyalty-building guidelines for effective coaching:

- Recognize a job well done.

- Ask permission to share insights.

- Declare your intent.

- Be positive and encouraging.

- Share information that helps people make better choices.

RECOGNIZE A JOB WELL DONE

People will be more open to our insights and coaching if we begin by letting them know we respect and recognize the good work they are already doing. "You do great work here." This feedback has to be honest and genuine, but doesn't need to be lengthy.

ASK PERMISSION TO SHARE INSIGHTS

Something as simple as "Would it be OK for me to share a thought with you?" can be a good icebreaker. It's often also better than "Can I give you some feedback?" since some people view the idea of "feedback" as negative or critical. Asking permission shows respect and allows the other person to tell us if they are busy right now and when they will be free.

DECLARE YOUR INTENT

State up front that you just want to share an idea to help them, not to criticize them in any way. "I just want to be helpful. I noticed something in your conversation with Ms. Sadek and want to share this thought with you. Is that OK? Is now a good time?"

BE POSITIVE AND ENCOURAGING

Our tone of voice and body language needs to be warm and welcoming. As we discussed in Chapter 7, the other person should feel we are on their side and only interested in their continued success. They should feel the Three Core Loyalty Principles of empathy, responsibility, and generosity from us.

SHARE INFORMATION THAT HELPS PEOPLE MAKE BETTER CHOICES

An effective way of doing this is to ask thoughtful questions. "How do you feel that conversation went with Ms. Sadek? I wonder if there was a different way to handle her frustration with the pedometer. What do you think?" Give the other person an opportunity to share their observations and feelings. Then, after listening to learn and showing empathy for their situation, share the insight you feel may be helpful.

Coaching to attain loyalty takes practice. Very simply, we want anyone we coach to walk away feeling, "He really cares about me and was really thoughtful to share that with me."

Here is another example of a manager coaching an employee—this time in a hospital. Jan is the manager of the Labor and Delivery Ward at the hospital. Andrea is an OB tech. As you read their conversation below, note whether each guideline draws from the principles and practices of leading loyalty.

JAN: Andrea, how's your day?

ANDREA: (perky) Just great so far.

JAN: We like the work you've been doing since you joined the team last month. You're a great OB tech. Do you remember I said we'd be having one-to-one talks now and then? Would this be a good time to talk?

ANDREA: Sure.

JAN: The shift Thursday night—it was crazy, wasn't it? There was an emergency C-section in Room 2 and most of us had to rush in and help. And then there was Mr. Kim in Room 3, and his wife wasn't progressing well. Do you recall he asked you to come in and help her?

ANDREA: (defensive) Yes, but I was busy stocking the carts.

JAN: Well, he got quite upset. Can you tell me what happened?

ANDREA: I was stocking the epidural carts because they were empty from the rush we had. And this guy came out and shouted at me that I was standing around doing nothing while his wife was dying.

JAN: Wow. That sounds stressful.

ANDREA: It was! She wasn't dying, and I told him so. There wasn't anything I could do for her anyway. So I told him to be patient because we had an emergency in the next room and the nurses would get to her.

JAN: Tell me more.

ANDREA: He stormed off and said he was going to complain to management about this lousy hospital and the help and everything about me and my lazy, good-for-nothing attitude.

JAN: That's frustrating.

ANDREA: I just ignored him. I'm not sure if that was the right thing to do.

JAN: Do you think you should've handled it differently?

ANDREA: Yes, but I'm not sure how. I really couldn't do anything for her. I'm not a nurse!

JAN: I understand. You must have felt pretty overwhelmed. Would you mind if I share a thought with you?

ANDREA: Sure.

JAN: In those situations, I always think first of the empathy principle. Remember the huddle we had when we talked about empathy and the skills involved to show it?

ANDREA: Yes, first make a genuine human connection.

JAN: How do you think you could have done that with Mr. Kim?

ANDREA: I don't know. Maybe I could have stopped stocking the cart to talk with him.

JAN: That's where empathy starts, and it's just that simple. Sometimes when we're really busy, it's hard to make that human connection. But the more you work on it, the more it turns into a habit. And then, just listen. Sometimes when patients like the Kims are upset, they just want someone to hear them out.

ANDREA: You mean just stop and listen?

JAN: Yes. It can be that simple—just a listening ear. As you listen, you start understanding the real problem. You can learn about the real job to be done.

ANDREA: Right. I remember that now.

JAN: So, what do you think was the real job to be done?

ANDREA: Take a minute to just give both of them some reassurance? Maybe get her a drink of water or another blanket?

JAN: It might have been as simple as that. I don't think they really expected you to deliver her baby painlessly right there and then. What they really needed was some empathy—somebody to let them know they weren't forgotten. That's a job we can all do.

ANDREA: But what about the epidural carts?

JAN: What do you think?

ANDREA: Well, I guess around here it's always a balancing act.

JAN: (laughs a little) Isn't that the truth.

ANDREA: But I could have taken a moment to help Mrs. Kim and still gotten everything done with the carts. I can see that now.

JAN: Yeah, I think you're right. And you know what? You're going to do just fine here, Andrea. I'm glad you're on my team.

ANDREA: Thanks. Me, too.

What impact do you think this style of coaching had on not only addressing the problem, but engendering real loyalty toward Jan and the hospital? As you can see from the table below, Jan drew from each of the Three Core Loyalty Principles and put many of the key practices into play:

Core Principle	Key Behavior	How Jan Built Loyalty as a Coach
Empathy	Make a Genuine Human Connection	• Began the conversation by asking how Andrea was doing. • Sincerely complimented Andrea and let her know she was aware of her contributions since joining the team. • Asked if "now" was a good time to talk—she's respectful of Andrea's time. • Empathized with the stress of having Mr. Kim come in and yell at her. • Ended the conversation by sharing how much she appreciated Andrea and was glad she was on her team.
Empathy	Listen to Learn the Hidden Story	• Although she had many of the "facts" about the Thursday night shift, asked for Andrea's account. • Prompted Andrea to keep sharing by asking her to "tell me more" instead of jumping in to solve the problem.
Generosity	Share Insights Openly	• Asked Andrea, "Would you mind if I share a thought with you?" • Reinforced understanding when Andrea correctly assessed the situation.
Responsibility	Follow Up to Strengthen the Relationship	• Took responsibility in following up with Andrea and strengthened their relationship in the process.
Responsibility	Discover the Real Job to Be Done	• After exploring the situation together, asked Andera directly, "What do you think was the real job to be done?" giving Andrea the opportunity to own the solution.

As you think about your team, how often are you sharing insights, as Jan did with Andrea, to help others get better? As a loyalty leader, this is some of the most important work you can do to foster loyalty from team members and customers alike.

How about sharing insights with a business you love to perhaps help them get better? This is what generous people do. Our friend Laing shares this story about her experience with a local women's clothing boutique:

> **My friends and I were really torn about this place because, while we loved the clothing she carried, the owner was a nightmare to deal with. Many of us stopped going there. One day I decided to approach her and was very frank, although I did my best to speak in a kind and compassionate way so as not to offend her. I told her how much I loved her merchandise, but it was hard dealing with her. I shared that she should acknowledge people when they walk in and be more friendly and engaging, make eye contact, connect with us. I think she figured she had such cool stuff, she didn't need to make any effort at all. I am happy to report that our little chat seems to have worked. This place is a lot more fun to visit now, and I've ended up buying more, too!**

A low-risk way to develop our Loyalty Leader Mindset and practice sharing insights openly is to talk with people who could use some coaching at a business we visit as a customer. Follow the guidelines in this chapter by first recognizing what they do well, ask permission to share your thoughts, declare your intent to help them, be positive, and share your insight in as kind and generous a way as possible. Like most things, the more we practice this key behavior, the more confident we will become in sharing our insights with the people we work with every day.

LEADER APPLICATION—THE PRACTICE OF SHARING INSIGHTS OPENLY

If you model effective teaching and coaching, the team will learn it from you. You want them to become active teachers and coaches themselves. When you coach them, let them know they will be expected to coach each other, so they should pay close attention. Teach them the guidelines so they will know what to do. Make sure they know that coaching based on the core principles and practices of loyalty is not criticism—it's about sharing insights. Give them opportunities to practice coaching and share insights with each other.

Rob Markey of Bain & Company, a globally respected authority on customer loyalty, believes "the key to success in empowering frontline employees lies in giving them a framework within which to operate and feedback about how they are performing within that framework. Help them become self-directing and self-correcting as they work toward a clear, understandable outcome."[2] In other words, teach the team the Three Core Loyalty Principles and then constantly share thoughts with them about getting better at applying the key practices of each. Focus everybody's attention on one outcome: creating more truly loyal customers.

At American Express, there was a time when their team at the service-operations call center was dealing with millions of calls a year, and the reps were monitored on how long each call took and whether they followed the script exactly. Management was totally focused on controlling costs. But when they shifted their focus to increasing customer loyalty, everything changed. They made their key success measure "the enthusiastic recommendations of card members." They got rid of the scripts and the time limits. Instead, they coached the service team on loyalty guidelines and let them use their own judgment within those guidelines. The result? Their costs actually went down under the new system as the employees took ownership and shared insights on how to resolve common customer issues. Best of all, American Express saw a 10 to 15 percent increase in customer spending and a big drop in customer churn.

Why did they get this result? In Markey's words, "Because employees are deeply involved in figuring out how to meet fundamental business objectives." Their brains are engaged. Their contribution means something. They're not just robots at the end of a phone line. Managers don't dictate how team members reach the objectives, but they do give them plenty of coaching and input on the loyalty guidelines. Markey suggests that managers should do these three things:

1. Set in place "a framework within which your employees can succeed." (For us, that means the Three Core Loyalty Principles and their associated practices.)

2. Give the team "a clear measure of success." (For us, that means a rising number of loyal customers.)

3. Give team members "fast, frequent, and simple feedback to help them learn." (For us, that's sharing insights openly to help everyone win. These insights can come from simply observing what's going on, from customer surveys, or from following up with customers to learn what could have been done better.)

The result, according to Markey: "Dramatically lower employee attrition, lower costs, and higher customer loyalty. In short, strategic and financial success."[3]

HUDDLE 9—SHARE INSIGHTS OPENLY

Generously communicate our thoughts, feelings, knowledge, and concerns.

1. **CELEBRATE**

   Celebrate someone who was generous to a customer or team member.

2. **LEARN**

   Discuss the following questions:

   a. Describe a time when a customer or team member shared an insight that was helpful.

   b. How effective are we at sharing insights with each other now?

   c. Which of the guidelines for sharing insights do we need to improve on?

   d. Who on our team is a great example of coaching?

3. **COMMIT**

   Share insights openly to help the team.

4. **SCHEDULE FOLLOW-UP**

   Huddle 10 date/time? Who will lead?

CHAPTER 10

SURPRISE WITH UNEXPECTED EXTRAS

"MAKE UNEXPECTED SURPRISES A ROUTINE PART OF
HOW YOU SERVE YOUR CUSTOMERS, AND THEY'LL
SPREAD THE LOVE."
—JOHN JANTSCH

MODEL . TEACH . REINFORCE

One of our clients told us this story:

> Several years ago, our family dog was acting ill, and we took
> him to the veterinarian. We got the devastating news that
> our dog had cancer that was well advanced and that he

> would not recover. We were crushed. The staff at the animal hospital was overwhelmingly kind, and it was clear they knew how difficult this was for us. After the diagnosis, one of the technicians took Milo for a few minutes and brought him back wrapped in a blanket. We said our goodbyes. A few days later, we got a package in the mail. In those few minutes with Milo, they had taken a picture and an imprint of our dog's paw, framed them, and sent the gift to us along with a note of condolence. It meant so much to our grieving little family.

What kind of people work at this veterinary clinic? What principles do they live by? Think of the impact they had as they demonstrated not only intense empathy, but also surprised the family with an extra gift that went far beyond what was expected.

In building loyalty, there are few spotlights as bright as the unexpected extras that make customers smile, glow, and rave about us. Similarly, there are few things that engage and excite team members as much as when they feel the delight of a customer. Sending personal messages, remembering names, experimenting with surprising new service ideas—these simple gestures endear us to customers and increase their loyalty. And they also bring meaning and joy to the work we do each day.

WHAT DOES SURPRISING WITH UNEXPECTED EXTRAS LOOK LIKE?

Consider this story about a pizza restaurant that was a little unusual. Actually, it was *very* unusual. Of the hundreds of identical stores in this pizza chain, this one produced the most revenue and had the lowest staff turnover. The executives of the company put the place under a microscope to find out what made it so different. It turns out it was a manager who engendered deeply loyal customers and crew.

Like many such places, this restaurant was staffed by teenagers and college kids out to earn a few bucks. They showed up, put on an apron, did their job, and went home. Usually, the turnover in this type of business is sky-high—it's only a temporary job, after all. There is little loyalty and practically no commitment, and no one expects anything different. But when this particular manager's team started a shift, they formed a huddle. They'd be leaning in, standing up, climbing on a bench, talking excitedly, while the manager wrote things down rapidly. This manager is extraordinary in one respect. As he huddles with his team, he asks only one question: *"What can we do for our customers this week that we've never done before?"*

The question, all by itself, excites his team. They are smart people, and he wants the benefit of their brains, not just their hands. The huddle is an opportunity for brainstorming ideas that are way outside the box (or *pizza* box, if you will), and the manager gleefully sends them off to try out their ideas. Here are just a few:

One team member liked eating cold pizza for breakfast. It occurred to him that others might, too. "How about it?" he asked the huddle one evening. The next morning he and another employee cruised the bus stops around town, selling leftover pizza to the people waiting for a bus. Somewhat surprised but pleased, the customers ate it up (literally and figuratively). Soon, the team members were selling boxes full of cold pizza every morning.

A second idea focused on the fact that every afternoon at about the same time, the restaurant experienced a rush of customers heading home from work and stopping for a takeout pizza. This was frustrating for both the employees who were suddenly overwhelmed with work and the customers who had to wait in line. While brainstorming in the huddle, one employee (who was a car-racing fan) came up with the idea of turning the restaurant parking lot into a pit stop for drive-by customers. The idea was to serve customers in their cars as quickly as possible instead of forcing them to come into the takeout counter. They formed four-member teams and raced around taking orders and credit cards, pulling hot pizza boxes off an assembly line and moving cars through the line quickly. The customers loved it. Every day, employees clocked themselves to see how much faster they could put a hot pizza into the hands of an arriving customer. The manager would stand outside laughing and timing them with a stopwatch. It turned into a high-energy competition to dream up new ways of doing the job even faster.

Another idea that came out of the huddle centered around a team member who noticed the laundry chute in his house where he dropped his clothes. He thought, "Why not a pizza chute?" The idea was to slide pizzas at high speed from the kitchen to the parking lot, eliminating the need to run into the store and back. But how to make it work? Eventually they got a long plastic waterslide from a carnival and ran it through a window from the ovens in the kitchen to the pit crew outside. Soon they were sliding pizza boxes down the chute from storefront to parking lot, thus cutting precious seconds and hassle for their patrons. Now customers could text ahead exactly what they wanted, and their fresh, hot pizza was waiting for them curbside when they arrived.

In each of the team's huddles, members talked about what was working, then proposed wild new experiments and made plans to carry them out. When something worked, they celebrated like crazy. Customers loved the place and were always looking forward to the next innovation. This unique pizza franchise had become predictably unpredictable in a good way.

The manager's technique for earning loyalty was disarmingly simple: "What can we do for our customers this week that we've never done before?" The question energized his team, engaged their minds, and excited their hearts. No wonder turnover was so low! The staff didn't just *like* working there, they *loved* it. The manager's application of the generosity principle was simple: Surprise with unexpected extras by constantly experimenting with new and creative ways to show people you care.

COUNTERFEIT SURPRISE WITH AN UNEXPECTED EXTRA

A counterfeit "extra" is giving something that customers already expect, like a fortune cookie at the end of a Chinese dinner or the sample box of floss from the dentist. Customers aren't surprised and delighted by "extras" like these. If we want to increase loyalty through living the principle of generosity, we need to do better than that. Of course, the last thing customers want is to be surprised by an unpleasant extra expense. A friend shared this example:

> I walked into a do-it-yourself copy store to print some copies of a presentation I was going to give. Over the copy machines hung a sign: *Because of the large number of errors made by customers, we will be unable to cover the cost of these errors in the future. You are limited to one error, and you will be charged for any errors after that.* I shrugged and started the copy machine. I was annoyed when the first copy came out on the wrong size of paper. So I adjusted the settings to

> the correct size. My second try was also on the wrong size of paper. *Well, I'll be paying for that one,* I thought to myself. I "adjusted" it again. I ended up making seven more bad copies as I tried repeatedly to resize the paper. Exasperated, I asked the attendant for help. She looked at the copy machine and found that it had been set incorrectly. She kindly fixed the problem for me. When I went to pay for my copies, however, I was surprised to find that the helpful attendant charged me for eight of the nine bad ones! "I thought you said there was something wrong with the setup on your machine," I objected.
>
> "Sorry," the woman answered, clearly uncomfortable with charging me. She pointed apologetically at the notice hanging over my head. "It's our policy. I guess you should've asked for help sooner." I shook my head and paid for the copies. At 10 cents per bad copy, I was out only 80 cents. But I left that store in a cranky mood and never went back.

That big, threatening sign at this copy center symbolized a "customer beware" mindset, the exact opposite of a generosity mindset. The provider should be doing everything possible to ensure that customers never have to bear the cost of a mistake. But instead of making our friend's experience pleasant, the copy store made it unpleasant. They traded 80 cents for the customer's loyalty—penny-wise and pound-foolish.

In another example, our friend Fred Reichheld was hampered by a traffic jam and got to the airport an hour late for returning his rental car. There were some nasty surprises in store for him. (Note that this is not the company where Sandy worked.) He explained:

> First, for the one extra hour we used the car, the rental agency charged us 50 percent of the cost of an additional day. Wouldn't 1/24th make more sense? Then it added on a charge of almost $75 because the tank was only half full. The employee who checked us in was obviously embarrassed by these unreasonable fees.[1]

The company might make money off an unpleasant surprise (Reichheld calls this kind of revenue "bad profits"), but it stresses out the frontline employees and drives customers away.

WHY DON'T WE SURPRISE WITH UNEXPECTED EXTRAS?

First, it takes extra effort to think about ways to delight customers and put them into practice. There's the excuse that "I'm already too busy with the work I'm doing to take on this extra surprise stuff." Fortunately, we don't buy it. The extra energy it takes to do little things to let people know you value them is more likely to energize you than wear you down. Simple things like remembering customers' names and any details shared during their last visit can surprise and delight them. Personal handwritten thank-you notes can go a long way to let people know how much you value them, and they don't take very long to write.

Second, some organizations have policies that *prevent* employees from being generous, like the copy-store and car-rental examples described above. Imagine how many times an employee has to deliver bad news to a customer, knowing that the customer will be disappointed, upset, or angry. Requiring employees to enforce ungenerous policies is a surefire way to undermine the loyalty of both customers and employees. Like peering into a microscope, customer-facing employees see close-up the kinds of problems customers have and can use their magnified vision to identify opportunities for making the customers' experience better. As McKinsey researchers pointed out:

> **Engaging with customers is still undertaken largely through personal contact. And there's no shortcut to creating emotional connections with customers; it requires ensuring that every interaction is geared toward leaving them with a positive experience. That takes more than great products and services—it takes motivated, empowered frontline employees. Creating great customer experiences requires having an engaged and energized workforce, one that can translate individual experiences into satisfying end-to-end customer journeys and can continue to improve the journeys to maintain a competitive edge.[2]**

In other words, it's vital to focus on "improving the customer journey." So how do we motivate and empower customer-facing employees to improve the customer's end-to-end experience? It's incredibly simple: Ask for their ideas!

HOW DO WE SURPRISE WITH UNEXPECTED EXTRAS?

It's easy. First, brainstorm ideas with your team, then run thoughtful experiments to see what works. Many of the great customer-service ideas at Enterprise Rent-A-Car—from giving customers a cold bottle of water on a hot day to picking up customers from their home, office, or repair shop—came from the bottom up. These ideas weren't dreamed up in the corporate tower. They came from empowered frontline branch employees and local general managers exploring new ways to make the rental experience easier and better for customers. A form of "Darwinism"—variation and selection—is at work across the thousands of Enterprise branches. Employees try different ways to make the customer experience better (variation), and those that work get noticed by other branches and adopted there, too (selection).

Brainstorm with your team. Ask them, "What could we do for customers that we have never done before to make their experience better? How could we exceed customer expectations and show customers how much we really care about them?" To generate ideas, think about things that potentially annoy or stress out customers or waste their time. When do customers hesitate or look confused? What questions do clients ask that they shouldn't have to ask? What would make them feel more valued and appreciated? These things do not need to cost a lot of money. In fact, some of the best ideas don't cost anything. Fred Reichheld refers to inexpensive little ways to delight customers as "frugal wows."

For successful brainstorming, there should be lots of diverse viewpoints in the conversation. If two people have the same opinion, one is unnecessary. So invite your entire team, and maybe include people from another department or those with different roles. And be sure to include those who interact with customers most often.

One caution: Most brainstorming sessions are too tame. These should be storms, not drizzles. Too often, a brainstorming session is a group of people who sit down together, list a few ideas, and then argue about them. No brainstorming session is worth doing unless the ideas fly fast and free. Here are some guidelines to make brainstorming exciting and fun enough to produce the kind of ideas that will incite real loyalty:

- Write ideas down *fast* on a chart or whiteboard.
- *Don't judge* the ideas at this stage. Just write them down quickly.

- Ask the group for *lots* of ideas. Go for quantity, not quality.

- Keep it high-energy. Nobody relaxes. Try standing instead of sitting. Encourage wild ideas and build off them.

- If the idea flow starts to slow down, try asking these questions:

  - "What are the real jobs our customers want us to do for them?"

  - "Let's walk through everything our customers do with us. Where could we make their 'journey' easier and better?"

  - "What would it take to ensure that *all* of our customers love us?"

  - "Where are we not as good as our competitors? What could we do to close the gap?"

  - "Suppose our customers could completely serve themselves. What would we do to help them?"

  - "If we could read our customers' minds, what are they thinking about us? What should we change?"

  - "We're customers, too. What would we want if we were doing business with our team?"

Most important, have fun with it! In just five minutes, a team can toss out dozens of ideas. While there may be some that won't work, others could be pretty good, and a few might be great. But the benefits of brainstorming go beyond the ideas. Team members feel heard, valued, connected, and aligned. They feel involved—part of the solution. Further, knowing that these brainstorming sessions will be held regularly encourages preparation. Team members can prepare for these discussions by:

- Listening to customers to discover the real jobs they are trying to get done.

- Following up with customers and asking what we could have done better.

- Reading customer-survey results, and customer comments online.

- Researching ideas. How are other companies like ours attracting loyal customers? How about companies that are *not* like ours?

- Identifying any "nasty surprises" that upset customers. How can we avoid them?

- Looking for ways to simplify the customer experience and make it easier for them to work with us.

Once the fast-and-furious brainstorming session is complete, ask team members to go up to the whiteboard or flip chart where the ideas are written down, and make up to three checkmarks by the ideas they like best. Give each person a different color marker if there are any concerns about "voter fraud." They can put all three of their votes on one idea or spread them across three different ideas. In evaluating which ideas to implement, ask whether the solution will make life easier for customers. That's what we saw the pizza place doing to great effect.

Then sort the ideas that get the most votes into two buckets: ideas your team could implement right now, and things that require management involvement before implementation (like a change in policy or pricing, a promotion, a system enhancement, a new investment, etc.).

Here are examples of ideas your team could potentially implement now:

- Send personal handwritten thank-you notes.

- Remember customer names, texting or emailing them on their birthdays.

- Welcome people with a small inexpensive gift—maybe a cookie, a flower, a cold water bottle, or even a glass of water.

A hotel team was concerned about disappointing guests when they requested a later checkout time but didn't want to pay extra for the room. The front-desk employees began discovering some of the jobs these guests wanted to get done by checking out later: "If you don't mind me asking, sir, what is the reason for needing to stay in your room until 2 p.m.? Perhaps there is something else we could do to accommodate your needs?" Sometimes the guests needed a quiet place for an important conference call. Other times they wanted to work out in the fitness center before departing the hotel and needed a place to shower and change. The front-desk team was able to provide a quiet room for the phone call and access to the changing room in the fitness center after checkout time to meet the guests' needs.

These are examples of the "frugal wow"—little things that don't cost much but make customers happy, especially if they demonstrate empathy, responsibility, and generosity. They amount to easy wins that ultimately strengthen the relationship. Even if little extras for customers cost money (like the replacement tube of toothpaste the housekeeper left in the guestroom), consider it money well spent if it helps you create more promoters.

Your team will undoubtedly come up with ideas that require management involvement. Disney is famous for exciting spectacles, but at one time, the Disney Store was just another retail store. The kids loved the products, but the stores themselves were nothing special. More recently, Disney completely redesigned the space with "pixie-dust trails" and a "magic mirror" to be "the best thirty minutes of a child's day."

Think about your team or organization, store or office—what's interesting about it? Look around at your space. Look at your online presence. Ask team members for their opinions. What could you do to make it more appealing, more of an "experience" for customers? What's the equivalent of "pixie-dust trails" or "magic mirrors" for your customers?

Whether it's free CrossFit and cardio classes at Athleta, yoga sessions at Lululemon, personal styling and beauty services at Nordstrom in West Hollywood, or enjoying an espresso and haircut at Frank And Oak in Toronto, many physical stores are shifting from driving transactions to building relationships. In other words, companies that are staying relevant are creating an experience for their customers that builds loyalty.

Run thoughtful experiments to see what works. From the list of ideas your team could implement right now, pick one and run an experiment. Organizations that build loyalty constantly experiment with new ways to show customers how much they are valued and appreciated.

Some years ago, a restaurant did an experiment to find out if giveaways made a difference to their customers. One day they greeted customers with a "thank you for coming" and offered either a free cup of yogurt or a small key chain. The next day there was no greeting and no gift. They kept up this alternating routine for several weeks. In the end, the researchers found that the combination of a greeting and a gift had a huge impact on what the customers spent: 46.4 percent more! In other words, customers who got a little unexpected extra—whether the yogurt cup or the key chain—ended up spending nearly half again more than the customers who didn't. Also, the gifted customers gave the restaurant much higher online recommendations. "The authors of this study conclude that retailers should greet customers who enter their stores and, if possible, provide a small gift."[3]

Of course, it doesn't have to be a gift or a freebie. The unexpected extra could simply be the time and effort that excite the customer's enthusiasm or relieve the customer of stress and hassle. Senator Bob Kerrey is often quoted as saying, "Unexpected kindness is the most powerful, least costly, and most underrated agent of human change." Here are some other examples.

- At the Ace Hardware store in Mequon, Wisconsin, employees greet you warmly, they learn your name, and they will give you a hand with any project. They will not only sell you a grill or a snowblower, they will deliver and put it together for you.[4]

- At Chick Fil-A, the location manager stops by each table and asks if she can refresh anyone's beverage. How often does this happen to you at a fast-food chain?

- On Southwest Airlines, flight attendants sometimes tell jokes or sing the safety announcement, sharing their musical or comedy gifts with passengers.

- Bose Corporation provides a number of short how-to videos to answer common customer questions about speakers, thus saving both the customer and themselves a lot of time and trouble.

Unexpected extras don't have to be complicated or expensive. Fun ideas like a pizza chute or simple ones like a cold bottle of water on a hot day can make a big difference over time. "From handwritten notes to just-baked cookies, a simple gesture can go a long way toward shoring up customer loyalty in a competitive marketplace," says entrepreneurship expert Scott Gerber. "Even just a quick phone call can do more to earn your customers' long-term trust than any coupon or discount code—really."[5]

So try the ideas your team is excited about. Do them on a small scale so the risks are minimal. See what works. Then celebrate like crazy when an idea works. Our colleague Jill Peterson shared this story:

> I usually hate renting cars when I travel to the LAX airport. However, the last time I flew there, I thought I would try Enterprise, and to my surprise, it was an unexpected, delightful experience. The line was long when we walked in, but they moved us through quickly and got me outside to choose the car I would be driving. As the associate was walking around the car with me to make sure it was in good shape, she pleasantly asked me the standard questions one gets asked when renting a car. And then came the shining, very unexpected moment: She said, just as I was getting into the driver's seat: "Here is my business card. If you have any issues with this car, my cell number is here, and you can call or text me and I will make sure you get taken care of." *What?* She gave me her personal cell number in case I had a problem with my rental car! I was blown away. Did I need to get in touch with her while I was in L.A.? No. But this little gesture sure gave me the peace of mind that I could if anything had gone wrong.

We don't know whether this practice of handing out personal business cards to car renters is a small-scale branch experiment or a new chainwide customer-service initiative. Regardless, it is certainly a generous, unexpected surprise likely to create even more Enterprise promoters.

LEADER APPLICATION— THE PRACTICE OF SURPRISING WITH UNEXPECTED EXTRAS

As with all of the loyalty practices, it's critical that, as leaders, we model the behavior we wish to see from others. The generosity we show directly impacts how our employees treat our customers. Associates look to their leaders to see what the norm is and what is valued in the organization. Again, leaders create culture. Surprise your team members with unexpected extras—free or low-cost. Send birthday cards, bring in bagels, or give a little gift card. Celebrate every time an employee does something to create another customer promoter.

Meet regularly with your team to brainstorm. Make it a priority. Foster diverse viewpoints, encourage participation, and reassure your team that all ideas are welcome. Don't be afraid to experiment. Follow through with implementing the best ideas, and iterate to improve. Then celebrate like crazy if an idea works.

Trust and empower your team members to decide when to give a customer an "unexpected extra." Consider providing your people with resources they can use at their discretion as they work to build customer loyalty. The Ritz-Carlton gives every employee discretion to spend up to $2,000 to make a customer happy. This is an extreme example, but this policy is completely aligned with their philosophy that "at The Ritz-Carlton, we are ladies and gentlemen serving ladies and gentlemen." Might your employee make a mistake from time to time? Count on it. But chalk those up to learning and guide your team on how to make a better choice next time.

Finally, examine your policies to ensure they are not creating a system that brings "bad profits"—the $75 charge to refill half of the rental-car gas tank that would only cost $20 at the gas pump. We never want our team members to be in the unfortunate position of having to face down a customer over a policy that leaves both feeling dissatisfied. If your work to increase customer loyalty is encumbered by ungenerous policies, take responsibility for bringing this to the attention of your senior leadership and help them to find a better way.

HUDDLE 10—SURPRISE WITH UNEXPECTED EXTRAS

Experiment with new and creative ways to show people we care.

1. **CELEBRATE**

   Celebrate someone who shared insights to help a team member.

2. **LEARN**

   Discuss the following questions:

   a. When have we been surprised with an unexpected extra?

   b. What have we done to delight our customers?

   c. What extras can we come up with to surprise customers?

   d. How can we make life easier or more interesting for customers?

3. **COMMIT**

   Identify something new to surprise and delight customers.

4. **SCHEDULE FOLLOW-UP**

   Huddle 11 date/time? Who will lead?

PART
FIVE

IMPLEMENTING LOYALTY

CHAPTER 11

YOUR LEGACY AS A LOYALTY LEADER

"A LEGACY IS A GIFT TO THE FUTURE AND A GIFT TO THE PRESENT. IT IS THE CORE OF WHO YOU ARE—WHAT YOU STAND FOR, HOW YOU TREAT OTHERS, AND WHAT YOU CONTRIBUTE TO THE WORLD AROUND YOU."

—BARBARA GREENSPAN SHAIMAN

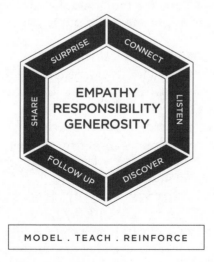

Someday you will leave the job you're in now. How do you want to be remembered? What do you want people to say about you? How will things be different because you were there? In other words, what *loyalty legacy* do you want to leave?

A delivery-room nurse was standing in line at a coffee shop when a woman approached her with a small child in tow. The woman said to her, "I carry a picture of you in my wallet."

"A picture of me?" the nurse asked, surprised.

"Five years ago, my son was born premature, and you were his nurse in the newborn ICU." She held up the little boy and continued, "You helped save my son's life, and I'll be forever grateful."

At that, the woman showed the nurse a tattered photo of herself with the baby. Both women wept. Reflecting on this experience, the nurse had this to say:

> **We never really know the impact we have on people, and this is something that I think about with every interaction I have throughout the course of the day. A warm, sincere greeting or smile may make a lasting impression on a visitor in the elevator who has just learned of her terminal diagnosis. Taking the time to sit with an employee who just needs to talk may help that person with a significant personal problem. Congratulating a co-worker on her son's recent accomplishment at school may make her day that much brighter. These are the moments that define who we are as leaders. These are the seeds of our legacy.[1]**

What seeds of your legacy are you planting today? Your legacy is about the memories you leave with people and the satisfaction you feel every day as you strive to create loyalty. Consider the legacy you're *already* creating with your customers and coworkers. Will they have outstanding memories of you connecting with them, listening to them, and caring enough to give them the help they really need? There are three kinds of legacy: a legacy of disloyalty, a counterfeit legacy, and a legacy of loyalty.

As we've seen, a legacy of disloyalty results from indifference to the needs of others, shrugging them off, or, even worse, dealing with them dishonestly. But it can also result from poorly chosen priorities: failing to emphasize loyalty, spending too much effort elsewhere, or mindlessly sticking to the rules at the expense of doing the right thing for another person.

A counterfeit legacy looks like empathy, but it's a façade. It looks like responsibility, but it's lip service instead of real service. It looks like generosity, but it's actually self-serving. Have you ever received good customer service, but just as you were leaving the location, the associate said something like, "You'll be receiving a survey. It would really help if you gave me the top score"? In attempts like these to "game" the survey, it makes us wonder if the employee's behavior is genuine or counterfeit. *Does the associate really care about me, or is this just about getting a top score?*

As business researcher and author Glenn Llopis wrote, to earn true loyalty:

> **You must know and be extremely connected with who you are and what you represent as an individual and a leader. What are the values and beliefs that influence how you lead, your behavior, and your attitude? In other words, it's all about who you are. It's about the principles you really believe in and really practice. What guiding principles can others expect from you? These principles should represent your most enduring ideas and ideals.[2]**

So our challenge is to do that—to adopt the Loyalty Leader Mindset and draw deeply from the wells of empathy, responsibility, and generosity. A wise writer, David Brooks, said:

> **About once a month, I run across a person who radiates an inner light. These people can be in any walk of life. They seem deeply good. They listen well. They make you feel valued. You often catch them looking after other people, and as they do so, their laugh is musical and their manner is infused with gratitude. They are not thinking about what wonderful work they are doing. They are not thinking about themselves at all.**
>
> **When I meet such a person it brightens my whole day. But I confess I often have a sadder thought: It occurs to me that I've achieved a decent level of career success, but I have not achieved that.[3]**

Like David Brooks, most of us have a ways to go before we "radiate an inner light." But that shouldn't discourage us. We can be more deeply good. We can listen better. We can make others feel more valued, and as we do so, become models of what it takes to earn the loyalty of others.

So who are you? Are you:

- The person who radiates an inner light—one who is deeply good, listens well, and makes other people feel valued?

- The fireman who goes back to mow the lawn of a man who just had a heart attack?

- The auto-glass repairman who creates a video in sign language to serve a hearing-impaired customer?

- The sales clerk who fills the real need—not just selling a young jobseeker a tie, but also coaching him on how to get the job?

- The cancer-ward nurse who helps a patient overcome self-pity by serving others?

If so, you are engendering the kind of loyalty that only comes through a legacy of service. Those who build lasting loyalty in their various customer relationships, both internal and external, have their priorities straight. Remember the Oracle study in our introduction: When asked what makes a memorable experience that causes consumers to stick with a brand, 73 percent of the people interviewed mentioned their experience with employees. Those who inspire true loyalty predominantly focus on the emotional intelligence of the heart.

Eminent psychologist Daniel Goleman said:

> **The most successful service reps are emotionally intelligent enough to assess a customer's emotions. They empathize and stay emotionally present to fine-tune their understanding of the customer's emotional needs [and to] find the best product or service for her needs, and the company sees increased customer engagement.**[4]

Employee engagement is about the heart, too. But in too many workplaces, there is no heart to be found. Employees feel little if any loyalty to their employers and have practically no emotional investment in their jobs. When asked about his airline's unusual record of success, Herb Kelleher of Southwest Airlines said it was because he always treats his employees like customers. He calls them his "inside customers." "When you treat them right, then they will treat your outside customers right. That has been a powerful competitive weapon for us."[5]

Jack Taylor, founder of Enterprise Rent-A-Car, had the same philosophy. Sandy shared: "When visiting rental branches, Jack frequently asked the employees he met if they were having fun. 'Jack, why aren't you asking them about their customer-service scores or their sales numbers?' And he explained, 'Because, Sport (Jack's friendly way of referring to me and others), if they're not having fun, nothing else really matters!'"

Throughout this book we have emphasized that loyal employees produce loyal customers. So, how do you win the hearts of employees, who in turn can win the hearts of customers? By modeling, teaching, and reinforcing the things we've been learning together in this book. It's the most important thing you can do to boost loyalty, and it costs very little. Armed with the loyalty principles, practices, and tools we've provided, you can build a legacy of loyalty.

That's why we invest so much in training people to use the principles, practices, and tools for building real loyalty. According to our valued client Cyndi Avery, director of human development at Grinnell Mutual insurance, the training embedded in the eleven huddles "is more than customer-service training; it is teamwork and leadership. It's even much more than that. It's about being a good person in general."

Perhaps the most valuable hands-on tool you can take away from this book is the loyalty huddle. You will see tremendous change in your team if you hold regular and frequent loyalty huddles based on the Three Core Loyalty Principles of empathy, responsibility, and generosity. When you've gone through all eleven chapters, start over. Make sure the entire team gets educated continually so the loyalty principles and practices become second nature. The more you hold the huddles, the more depth of discussion and action you'll get. As Seth Godin said: "This is where real impact happens: finding a cohort of people who want to change together. Organizing them and then teaching and leading them."[6]

True loyalty starts with you. A Loyalty Leader Mindset, based on the enduring principles of empathy, responsibility, and generosity, starts in your head. Then, as you live these principles each day, you teach others how to cultivate them in their hearts. As a result, employees will treat one another and customers the way they are treated. The old saying "Do unto others as you would have them do unto you" has extreme relevance today, says Professor Dave Ulrich. "Leaders who treat others with respect see it amplified throughout the organization. Leaders have to be the example of respect and character that others will follow."[7]

No matter where you are in your service journey, you are the model of a loyalty leader as of this moment. You are planting the seeds for your loyalty legacy now. So, let's start with a few basic challenges:

- How will you influence your team to hold the loyalty huddles?
- When will you hold your first huddle?
- How often will you hold the loyalty huddle? Weekly? Biweekly? Daily?
- Where will you hold the loyalty huddle?
- When are your best opportunities for coaching individuals?

OK. You have your plan. Now you can begin.

HUDDLE 11—YOUR LEGACY AS A LOYALTY LEADER

How do you want to be remembered by others?

1. **CELEBRATE**

   Celebrate someone with a great idea for delighting customers.

2. **LEARN**

   Discuss the following questions:

   a. How do we want to be remembered by others?

   b. Why do we need to "live" each of the Three Core Loyalty Principles?

   c. Who is a great example of leaving a loyalty legacy?

3. **COMMIT**

   Write down how you want to be remembered by others.

4. **SCHEDULE FOLLOW-UP**

   Huddle 12 date/time? Who will lead?

CHAPTER 12

SUSTAINING LOYALTY IN TEAMS AND ORGANIZATIONS

Throughout this book, we have shared the mindset and principles that create true loyalty and have illustrated how they are effective for every individual who interfaces with customers, both inside and outside an organization. We have also shown that the responsibility for creating loyalty is independent of title or position; often those who have the greatest impact on loyalty have the least formal authority.

We also recognize that many who will implement the principles and practices of loyalty will be leaders of frontline teams or even leaders of other leaders. For you, the focus is not only on implementing these principles, but on sustaining and continuously improving them as well. Achieving such a long-term objective is only possible if your team can translate these principles and practices into permanent habits of performance.

The framework for creating such habits of performance will be *The 4 Disciplines of Execution* (4DX), FranklinCovey's methodology for achieving goals that are "wildly important." We will use 4DX to give you a detailed execution plan, including the eleven loyalty huddles, and introduce you to a tool for capturing and assessing your progress: the 4DX Operating System (4DX OS). It has been our experience that this combination of methodology supported by technology will provide the visibility and accountability necessary to create lasting change. When used together with the Loyalty Leader Mindset and resulting principles and practices, you and your team will have a proven system for creating loyalty that is both consistent and sustainable.

DISCIPLINE 1: FOCUS ON THE WILDLY IMPORTANT

Discipline 1 is the discipline of focus. In the context of this book, the Wildly Important Goal (WIG) may seem obvious: *Create loyalty*. But real focus requires that you go further to not only define *what* you want to create, but also the level at which you want to create it and the date when you will reach that level. Without this clarity, your team will struggle to fully engage. Imagine running a race where the finish line is not clearly set—even if you love running, you won't get very far before you realize that something essential is missing: *the definition of winning.* The same is true with teams when the goal is not clear. No matter how deeply your team believes in the value of loyalty, their highest performance will only be delivered if the pursuit feels like a winnable game.

Answering the following questions will help you to create this level of focus:

- What will you measure?
- What is your starting line?
- What is your finish line?
- What is your deadline?

WHAT WILL YOU MEASURE?

Many of our clients have long-standing systems for measuring customer loyalty, and when they do, the loyalty score from these systems is the obvious choice for creating your WIG. However, it's important to ensure that the score you use relates directly to the aspect of loyalty you are seeking to improve. For example, if your customer-loyalty system measures multiple dimensions of the customer experience such as product quality, pricing, responsiveness to inquiries, and the pace of future innovations, the overall score may be too broad. A better option would be to use the score from only those items the principles of loyalty are targeted to impact.

If a customer-loyalty system isn't in place, you will want to choose a reasonable alternative to assess the level of loyalty your customers currently feel. For example, you could gather feedback from a sufficient sample of your customers through targeted surveys or phone conversations, or collect postings from customer-focused internet or social-media sites, or even create customer focus groups for direct interaction. Whatever method you choose, remember that being able to measurably track progress toward creating loyalty is a major factor in your team's engagement.

WHAT IS YOUR STARTING LINE?

Your team's success in creating loyalty will always be measured as progress *from your starting line.* With an existing system, this is usually the score on the most recent customer-loyalty assessment. However, if a system is not already in place, you may need to establish a starting line by making an educated assessment (based on the types of data described above) to score the level of loyalty your team is currently creating. Don't be overly concerned if you lack precision here—the number that matters most is next.

WHAT IS YOUR FINISH LINE?

This is the level of loyalty you are committing to achieve in your current phase. A note of caution: We often encounter leaders who believe in setting goals that are far beyond anything their team can achieve, while privately acknowledging that they'll be satisfied if they get 80 percent of the goal. This type of gamesmanship can significantly undermine your ability to drive engagement and results. Instead, set a goal for loyalty that challenges team members to rise to their highest level of performance, but which is also realistically achievable. In other words, create a WIG that is both *worthy* and *winnable*.

WHAT IS YOUR DEADLINE?

Simply put, this is the date on which you and your team will be accountable to have reached your finish line. In the language of the *4 Disciplines*, we refer to these elements as "From X to Y by When." Using this construct, your WIG for loyalty should be as simple and clear as this: "Improve customer loyalty from 47 to 61 by December 31."

With your WIG defined, your team now has a clear objective on which to focus—one that can be pursued beyond the day-to-day demands of your team's regular responsibilities. Like a compass, the WIG provides clear, consistent direction toward a level of loyalty that's *wildly important*. When your WIG is activated in 4DX OS, it might look like this:

WIGs	Leads	Commitments
48.00		‹ **Due This Week**
Customer Loyalty	Add Lead	(Jun 17, 2018 - Jun 23, 2018)
47.07		0% Kept
		New Commitment
Add WIG		

DISCIPLINE 2:
ACT ON THE LEAD MEASURES

Discipline 2 is the discipline of leverage. When we say "leverage," we mean investing your team's energy into the specific behaviors that have the greatest impact on loyalty. Lead measures are simply the "measures" of those powerful behaviors.

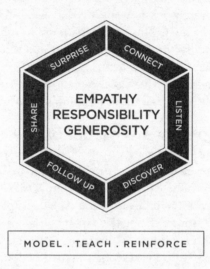

The Three Core Loyalty Principles are the true drivers of loyalty and should be used as your lead measures. In the simplest terms, your lead measures will be the number of times each week you and your team actually use these principles in interactions with your customers, either inside or outside your organization. Your reasoning here will be powerful to the team: *Understanding the principles of loyalty will only be valuable to the extent that we act on them; and the best way to ensure we act on them is to measure ourselves each week.*

We recommend that you create one lead measure for each of the Three Core Loyalty Principles. Remember, in loyalty huddles 2–4, you will focus on empathy, followed by responsibility in loyalty huddles 5–7, and finally, generosity in loyalty huddles 8–10.

When you activate your lead measures, your scoreboard might look like this:

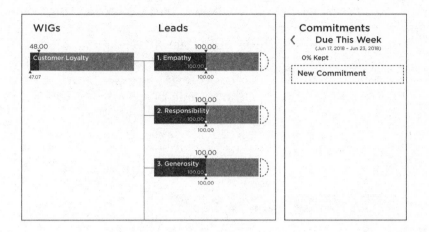

With a clearly defined WIG and lead measures that show your team members where to apply their greatest energy, you have answered two of the most important questions for high performance:

- WIG: *"What are we striving to achieve?"*

- Lead measures: *"How are we going to achieve it?"*

We believe that the simplicity and clarity of this plan can represent a new level in your ability to guide your team.

DISCIPLINE 3:
KEEP A COMPELLING SCOREBOARD

Discipline 3 is the discipline of engagement. It goes beyond the simplicity and clarity of Disciplines 1 and 2, and creates the greater outcome of enabling your team to take ownership over achieving loyalty.

Many leaders have felt the loneliness of being the only one who seems truly committed to achieving a goal. In fact, leadership can often seem like the ancient story of Sisyphus—you push a rock up a hill only to watch it roll back down, knowing that you will need to do it all over again tomorrow. But we invite you to think about the more important question: "Why is the *leader* the only one pushing the rock?" What if your entire team could be engaged in pushing the rock together? That's what happens when team members feel they are playing a game that belongs to them—*they play to win.*

To this end, the 4DX OS will give you a scoreboard designed to engage your entire team. Remember, however, that the discipline is not in creating the scoreboard itself, but in keeping the scoreboard compelling. You can only do this if the team sees the scoreboard as a guidance system for winning. For example, suppose you are holding loyalty huddle 3: Make a Genuine Human Connection with your team. Your scoreboard for the week might look like this:

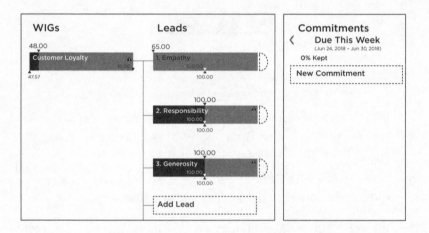

In the huddle, you bring to the surface that team members fell short of the number of interactions to which they had previously agreed. The visual display of the scoreboard makes the shortfall clear, and the color assignment (red) makes it feel urgent. As a leader, you can now focus all your energy on discussing *why* this happened rather than simply reporting the status. And, more important, you can engage your entire team in addressing the challenge with a unified focus to turn the red to green.

DISCIPLINE 4:
CREATE A CADENCE OF ACCOUNTABILITY

Discipline 4 is the discipline of accountability, and it ranks as the *single most important* discipline. Think of it this way: Disciplines 1, 2, and 3 are the design of a winnable game. But Discipline 4 is how you play that game. Without this discipline, there will always be something more urgent that will capture your attention and keep you from taking consistent action toward the WIG. We refer to this endless force of swirling demands as the *whirlwind*. You and your team live in that whirlwind every hour of every day. Inside the whirlwind, everyone will agree that loyalty matters and everyone will have the good intention to create it, but it will likely never happen—at least not at the level you hoped. Building loyalty will always be important, but it will never be urgent.

Discipline 4 breaks this cycle by asking you and your team to *personally commit* to the actions that will drive the score each week. By committing to a few small actions and consistently following through on them, your team will move the score and, more important, build a deeper sense of trust and respect for one another. When Discipline 4 becomes a permanent habit, you will have created a team that can not only execute, but will do so despite the pull of the day-to-day whirlwind.

Your greatest opportunity to build this discipline in your team is by leading impactful loyalty huddles. Most teams require about fifteen minutes to conduct a weekly loyalty huddle, and some find the focus and energy of the huddle so valuable that huddles start every day. The choice is up to you, but the minimum is once a week. If you allow more than a week to pass before reengaging your team members around loyalty, you'll likely find that the whirlwind has captured them once again.

The agenda for a loyalty huddle was covered in Chapter 1. Let's recap it here:

1. **CELEBRATE. Take a moment to recognize the performance of the team and any successes they've achieved. If warranted, highlight a particular individual on the team for his or her unique contribution that week.**

2. **LEARN. In the beginning, this can mean learning about a loyalty principle and discussing why the principle and practices are important. Once your team has fully absorbed the principle, learning can also include role-playing to build skill in using the principle, or brainstorming insights into where and how the team can improve.**

3. **COMMIT. Here, each member of the team offers a commitment for his or her part in creating loyalty this week. These commitments are made to you, as the leader; but, more important,**

the team makes them to one another. In this way, the commitments are more than professional—they become *personal*. The following week, this item will also include team members reporting whether they kept their commitments or not. This is an essential aspect of creating the sense of accountability you need for high performance. Remember that the team's primary role is to perform the lead measures. As a result, commitments should focus on how often and how well team members will perform them, as well as anything else they can do to improve performance.

4. SCHEDULE FOLLOW-UP. This final item includes confirming not only the day, time, and location of the next loyalty huddle, but also making assignments for which team member might lead the next week's discussion on a different principle.

The 4DX OS can provide powerful support to the cadence of your loyalty huddles. The clear display of your performance on lead measures, combined with progress on your WIG of loyalty, allows team members to celebrate when they are winning as well as diagnose where they fell short. But equally impactful is the ability to record commitments and track follow-through.

Let's take a look at a scoreboard when it includes commitments:

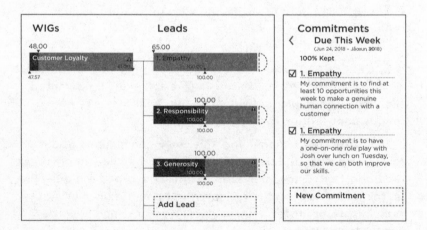

You can see from the above example that the commitments (on the right) include both the performance of the lead measure as well as improving a team member's skills. When the commitment is fulfilled during the week, the individual simply checks it off as complete. This real-time update can be performed through any PC, smartphone, or tablet offering an internet browser, or through the 4DX OS app (available on iPhone and Android).

When all of these elements are activated, 4DX OS enables you to answer the most critical questions for creating loyalty:

- How often are we consistently demonstrating the principles of loyalty in our day-to-day interactions with customers, both inside and outside our organization?

- Are those interactions increasing the level of loyalty indicated in the feedback from our customers?

- Are we following through on our commitments to drive loyalty, despite our whirlwind?

Creating real loyalty is a powerful destination in a journey of service—one that has the potential to transform leaders and teams, as well as entire organizations, careers, and lives. The loyalty mindset and principles are the guideposts along that journey. They point the way to leaving a legacy that can long outlast your tenure. *The 4 Disciplines of Execution*, along with the 4DX OS, are simply tools to enable you and your team to bring these powerful ideas to life, and to weave them into the permanent fabric of how your team achieves its mission.

SUSTAINING LOYALTY WITH MULTIPLE TEAMS

So far, we have intentionally focused on using *The 4 Disciplines of Execution* and the 4DX OS to create loyalty *through a single team*. However, it's worthwhile to address the perspective of senior leaders whose responsibility may be to lead multiple teams in a combined effort.

The 4DX OS provides many additional capabilities designed exclusively for the senior leader who must guide multiple teams. One of the most powerful of these is the Executive Scoreboard:

Name (leader's name)	WIG	Sub-WIG	Lead	Exclude	Commitments Kept	Commitments Made	Sessions Held	Sustainability Index	Commitment Quality
SE TEAM 1	43.24%	--	103.13%	□	100%	100%	100%	100%	14 days (Corey)
SE TEAM 2	111.4%	--	102.72%	□	100%	100%	100%	100%	4 days (Shaun)
Southeast Region	63.99%	10.95%	--	□	100%	100%	100%	100%	7 days (Corey)
Southeast Quality Control	114.48%	--	100%	□	100%	100%	100%	100%	--
NE Team 1	97.49%	--	103.28%	□	100%	100%	100%	100%	4 days (Shaun)
NE Team 2	133.63%	--	1742.81%	□	100%	100%	100%	100%	14 days (Corey)
NE Team 3	101.53%	--	96.36%	□	50%	100%	100%	83.33%	--
Northeast Region	143.65%	--	--	□	92.31%	100%	100%	97.44%	--
MW Team 1	150.00%	--	162.50%	□	100%	100%	100%	100%	4 days (Shaun)
MW Team 2	156.64%	--	108.42%	□	87.5%	100%	100%	95.83%	7 days (Don)
Midwest Region	96.12%	153.32%	--	□	89.47%	100%	100%	96.49%	7 days (Corey)
PAC Team 1	127.50%	--	113.13%	□	50%	100%	100%	83.33%	13 days (Don)
PAC Team 2	148.56%	--	93.75%	□	100%	50%	100%	83.33%	4 days (Shaun)
PAC Team 3	107.96%	--	106.88%	□	75%	100%	100%	91.67%	7 days (Krauf)
PAC Team 4	150.39%	--	137.50%	□	100%	100%	100%	100%	7 days (Krauf)
Pacific Region	111.81%	--	--	□	84%	90%	100%	91.33%	14 days (Don)
ABC Corporation	-20.74%	--	--	□	93.75%	100%	100%	97.92%	--
Averages	100.91%	67.9%	320.28%	□	91.83%	97.14%	100%	96.32%	8 days

SCORE	COLOR
6	
5	
4	
3	
2	
1	

Through this one report, which includes any or all teams across any time frame, you can monitor your teams' progress. In the above example, the seventeen teams listed (one per row) can be assessed in executing the principles and practices of loyalty, including:

- Which teams are succeeding at reaching their targeted level of loyalty (WIG), and which teams are behind pace.

- Which teams are using the loyalty principles (lead measures) at the targeted level, and which are falling short.

- Which teams are consistently holding their loyalty huddles, and which are not.

- Which teams are making commitments and following through on a personal level.

- Which are the top-ranked teams overall that should be recognized for their performance.

- Which are the lowest-ranked teams that may need additional coaching.

These are only a few of the insights that can be gained from this highly visual tracking tool. By simply clicking on each cell, you can go deeper to see trend information, moving averages, dates of loyalty huddles missed, team members who are failing to keep commitments, and many other insights that are vital to guiding multiple teams simultaneously. Our intention here is not simply to present the 4DX OS, but to show how essential these types of capabilities are for driving loyalty from the level of a senior leader.

Whether you are a leader of a frontline team or a leader of leaders, using the 4DX tools and methodologies can help operationalize the principles and practices of leading loyalty and support you in your personal journey toward leaving a loyalty legacy.

ENDNOTES

INTRODUCTION

1. Andrew Bary, "Everybody's Store," *Barron's*, February 13, 2007. Accessed June 8, 2018, https://www.barrons.com/articles/SB 117106869436404325.
2. Kate Taylor, "Costco Uses This Winning 6-part Formula That Makes It the Anti-Walmart," *Business Insider*, December 6, 2016. Accessed June 8, 2018, http://www.businessinsider.com/costco-formula-to -become-the-anti-walmart-2016-12.
3. Kris Hudson, "Costco's CEO Talks About Prices, Paychecks, and Prospects for Expansion," *Wall Street Journal*. Accessed June 10, 2009, http://wsjclassroom.com/archive/07dec/view_costco.htm.
4. Jeff Kober, World Class Benchmarking, February 8, 2017. Accessed June 8, 2018, http://worldclassbenchmarking.com/how-do-you-feel -about-customer-service/.

CHAPTER 1

1. North America Council | Coca-Cola Retailing Research Councils. Accessed June 8, 2018, http://www.ccrrc.org/councils/north-america/.
2. James Allen, Frederick Reichheld, and Barney Hamilton, "The Three 'D's' of Customer Experience," Harvard Management Update, November 7, 2005.
3. Werner Reinartz and V. Kumar, "The Mismanagement of Customer Loyalty," *Harvard Business Review*, July 2002. Accessed July 4, 2018, https://hbr.org/2002/07/the-mismanagement-of-customer-loyalty.
4. Ibid.
5. Matthew Dixon, Nick Toman, and Rick Delisi, *The Effortless Experience: Conquering the New Battleground for Customer Loyalty* (London: Penguin Group, 2013), 117.
6. Frederick F. Reichheld, "Loyalty-Based Management," *Harvard Business Review*, March–April 1993, https://hbr.org/1993/03/loyalty -based-management.

7. * Todd Kunsman, "Why Brand Ambassadors Could Be Your Best Marketing Strategy," business.com, December 26, 2017, https://www.business.com/articles/why-brand-ambassadors-matter-in-marketing/.

8. Randall Beck and Jim Harter, "Why Great Managers Are So Rare," Gallup.com Business Journal, March 25, 2014, http://www.gallup.com/businessjournal/167975/why-great-managers-rare.aspx.

9. Jim Collins, *Good to Great* (New York: Harper Business, 2001), 41, 194.

10. "The Secret to Delighting Customers: Putting Employees First," Avondale Business School. Accessed June 8, 2018, https://wp.avondale.edu.au/abs/2016/07/04/the-secret-to-delighting-customers-putting-employees-first/.

11. "Decoding Global Talent: 200,000 Survey Responses on Global Mobility and Employment Preferences," https://www.bcg.com. October 6, 2014. Accessed June 27, 2018, https://www.bcg.com/publications/2014/people-organization-human-resources-decoding-global-talent.aspx.

12. Annamarie Mann and Nate Dvorak, "Employee Recognition: Low Cost, High Impact," *Gallup Business Journal*, June 28, 2016, http://www.gallup.com/businessjournal/193238/employee-recognition-low-cost-high-impact.aspx.

13. Micah Solomon, "How to Win at Customer Service, Even If You're Not Nordstrom, Apple, or Amazon," *Forbes*, January 21, 2017, http://www.forbes.com/sites/micahsolomon/2017/01/21/how-to-compete-on-customer-service-when-youre-not-nordstrom-apple-or-amazon/#4e8bfe8344d8.

14. Peter Drucker, *Managing the Future* (New York: Routledge, 2016), 92.

15. Tania Tofoya, "LCL Client Interview." Telephone interview by author, June 6, 2017.

CHAPTER 2

1. Matthew Dixon, Nick Toman, and Rick DeLisi, *The Effortless Experience Conquering the New Battleground for Customer Loyalty* (New York: Portfolio/Penguin, 2013).

CHAPTER 3

1. Alexandra Robbins, "The Problem With Satisfied Patients," *Atlantic Monthly*, April 17, 2015, https://www.theatlantic.com/health/archive/2015/04/the-problem-with-satisfied-patients/390684/.

2. Viktor E. Frankl, *Man's Search for Meaning* (Boston: Beacon Press, 1992).

3. Jay Steinfeld, "Make Eye Contact With Your Customers Even When You're Not Face-to-Face," *CBS MoneyWatch*, September 1, 2010,

http://www.cbsnews.com/news/make-eye-contact-with-customers
-even-when-youre-not-face-to-face/.

4. Chi Kin (Bennett) Yim, David K. Tse, and Kimmy Wa Chan,
   "Strengthening Customer Loyalty Through Intimacy and Passion:
   Roles of Customer–Firm Affection and Customer–Staff Relationships
   in Services," *Journal of Marketing Research*, vol. 45 (2008) no. 6, 741.

CHAPTER 4

1. Lean Wen and Joshua Kosowsky, *When Doctors Don't Listen* (New
   York: St. Martin's Griffin, 2014), 7–8.
2. Dan Bobinski, "The Price of Poor Listening," Management-Issues.com,
   February 3, 1970. Accessed June 8, 2018, http://www.management
   -issues.com/opinion/6564/the-price-of-poor-listening/.
3. "The Costs of Poor Listening," Innolect, Inc. Accessed June 8, 2018,
   https://innolectinc.com/services-overview/the-cost-of-poor-listening/.
4. Christine M. Riordan, "Three Ways Leaders Can Listen with More
   Empathy," *Harvard Business Review*, November 2, 2014. Accessed June
   8, 2018, https://hbr.org/2014/01/three-ways-leaders-can-listen
   -with-more-empathy.
5. Peter Block, Walter Brueggemann, and John McKnight, *An Other
   Kingdom: Departing the Consumer Culture* (Hoboken, NJ: Wiley,
   2016), 72.
6. "Why Don't They Listen? A Universal Problem-Part II-
   Organizations, Management, & Healthcare," Confident Voices in
   Healthcare, November 3, 2014. Accessed June 8, 2018, http://www
   .confidentvoices.com/2014/10/30/why-dont-they-listen-a-universal
   -problem-part-ii-organizations-management-healthcare/.
7. Cited in Sarah Green, "Become a Better Listener," *Harvard Business
   Review Blog*, August 13, 2015, https://hbr.org/ideacast/2015/08
   /become-a-better-listener.html.
8. Lou Solomon, "The Top Complaints of Employees About Their
   Leaders," *Harvard Business Review*, June 24, 2015, https://hbr.org
   /2015/06/the-top-complaints-from-employees-about-their-leaders.

CHAPTER 5

1. "The Neurobiology of Giving Versus Receiving Support: The Role
   of Stress-Related and Social Reward–Related Neural Activity:
   Psychosomatic Medicine," LWW. Accessed July 16, 2018, https:
   //journals.lww.com/psychosomaticmedicine/Citation/2016/05000
   /The_Neurobiology_of_Giving_Versus_Receiving.7.aspx.

2. John G. Miller, *QBQ! The Question Behind the Question* (London: Penguin, 2004), 61.

3. Alex Rawson, et al., "The Truth About Customer Experience," *Harvard Business Review*, September 2013, https://hbr.org/2013/09/the-truth-about-customer-experience.

4. Matthew Dixon, Nick Toman, and Rick DeLisi, *The Effortless Experience Conquering the New Battleground for Customer Loyalty* (New York: Portfolio/Penguin), 2013.

5. Ibid.

6. Eric Almquist, John Senior, and Nicholas Bloch, "The Elements of Value," *Harvard Business Review*, September 2016, https://hbr.org/2016/09/the-elements-of-value.

7. Jacob Groshek, Chelsea Cutino, and Jill Walsh, "Customer Service on Hold: We Hate Phone Menus and Don't Trust Virtual Assistants like Siri," The Conversation, June 8, 2018. Accessed June 8, 2018, https://theconversation.com/customer-service-on-hold-we-hate-phone-menus-and-dont-trust-virtual-assistants-like-siri-51017.

8. Fred Reichheld, "It's All Lip Service Until You Measure It," LinkedIn, February 4, 2015, https://www.linkedin.com/pulse/best-advice-its-all-lip-service-until-you-measure-fred-reichheld?trk=mp-reader-card.

9. David Freemantle, *The Buzz: 50 Little Things that Make a Big Difference to Customer Service* (Boston: Nicholas Brealey Publishing, 2011), 12.

10. Jeff Haden, "Forget Customer Delight. Focus on Customer Relief," *Inc.*, Oct. 27, 2013, https://www.inc.com/jeff-haden/forget-customer-delight-focus-on-customer-relief.html.

11. Jim Harter, "Moneyball for Business: Employee Engagement Metanalysis," *Gallup Business Journal*, May 21, 2016, http://www.gallup.com/businessjournal/191501/moneyball-business-employee-engagement-meta-analysis.aspx?g_source=EMPLOYEE_ENGAGEMENT&g_medium=topic&g_campaign_tiles.

12. Stephen M. R. Covey, *The Speed of Trust* (New York: Free Press, 2006), 291.

13. Panisa Mechinda and Paul G. Patterson, "The impact of service climate and service provider personality on employees' customer-oriented behavior in a high-contact setting," *Journal of Services Marketing*, vol. 25 (2011): 2, 101–13.

CHAPTER 6

1. "Jobs to Be Done," Christensen Institute. Accessed January 21, 2017, http://www.christenseninstitute.org/key-concepts/jobs-to-be-done/.

2. Clayton M. Christensen, et al., "Know Your Customers' Jobs to Be Done," *Harvard Business Review*, September 2016, 56.

3. Retailtouchpoints, "My Last Great Customer Experience: 5 Ways REI Is Saving The Store," *The Retail TouchPoints Blog*, January 3, 2017. Accessed June 8, 2018, https://retailtouchpoints.tumblr.com/post /155344513667/my-last-great-customer-experience-5-ways-rei-is.

4. Cited in Micah Solomon, "Crafting a B2B Customer Experience," *Forbes*, January 11, 2014, https://www.forbes.com/sites/micahsolomon/2014 /01/11/crafting-a-b2b-customer-experience-like-an-expert/ #7d083c126f68.

5. Schon Beechler, "The Role of Leaders in Helping Others Find Meaning at Work," INSEAD Knowledge, December 13, 2013, http://knowledge.insead.edu/blog/insead-blog/the-role-of-leader s-in-helping-others-find-meaning-at-work-3055#comment-12301.

CHAPTER 7

1. Rebecca Wilson, "Why You Should Make Follow-Up a Priority," Marketing Profs, July 30, 2013, http://www.marketingprofs.com /articles/2013/11298/why-you-should-make-follow-up-a-priorit y-six-questions-and-five-tips.

2. William Grimes, "When Businesses Can't Stop Asking 'How Am I Doing?'" *New York Times*, March 16, 2012.

3. Vanessa K. Bohns, "A Face-to-Face Request Is 34 Times More Successful Than an Email," *Harvard Business Review*, January 26, 2018. Accessed June 8, 2018, https://hbr.org/2017/04/a-face-to-face -request-is-34-times-more-successful-than-an-email.

4. "Losing by Winning," *Seth's Blog*, February 5, 2017. Accessed June 8, 2018, https://seths.blog/2017/02/losing-by-winning/.

5. Fred Reichheld, *The Ultimate Question* (Brighton, MA: Harvard Business School Press, 2006), 66–67.

6. John Mehrmann, "10 Powerful Steps to Defuse Angry Customers," Business Know-How, n.d, http://www.businessknowhow.com /marketing/diffuse-anger.htm.

7. Gianfranco Walsh, Thorsten Hennig-Thurau, Kai Sassenberg, and Daniel Bornemann, "Does Relationship Quality Matter in E-services? A Comparison of Online and Offline Retailing," *Journal of Retailing and Consumer Services*, vol. 17, no. 2 (2010): 130–42. doi:10.1016/j. jretconser.2009.11.003.

8. Micah Solomon, "How Hospitality and Customer Service Experts Hire for Customer Service Positions," *Forbes*, November 7, 2014,

http://www.forbes.com/sites/micahsolomon/2014/11/07/avoid-hr
-carnage-by-learning-how-hire-for-customer-service/#56509d71165a.

CHAPTER 8

1. Christopher Elliott, "12 Ways to Annoy a Customer," *CBS MoneyWatch*, June 8, 2011, http://www.cbsnews.com/news/12-ways -to-annoy-a-customer/.

2. Sophie Bushwick, "Human First Response Is Generosity," *Scientific American*, September 19, 2012, https://www.scientificamerican.com /podcast/episode/human-first-impulse-is-generosity-12-09-19/.

3. Stephen Covey, *The 7 Habits of Highly Effective People* (London: Simon & Schuster, 1989).

4. Cited in Fred Kiel, *Return on Character: The Real Reason Leaders and Their Companies Win* (Brighton, MA: Harvard Business Press, 2015), 145.

5. Bill Taylor, "Trust Your Employees, Not Your Rulebook," *Harvard Business Review* blog, April 20, 2017, https://hbr.org/2017/04/trust -your-employees-not-your-rulebook?utm_campaign=hbr&utm _source=facebook&utm_medium=social.

6. Danny Meyer, *Setting the Table: The Transforming Power of Hospitality in Business* (New York: HarperCollins, 2009), 225.

7. Roger J. Dow, *Turned On: Eight Vital Insights to Energize Your People, Customers, and Profits* (New York: Harper Publishing, 1997), 30.

8. Leonard L. Berry, "How Service Companies Can Earn Customer Trust and Keep It," *Harvard Business Review*, April 19, 2017, https: //hbr.org/2017/04/how-service-companies-can-earn-customer-trust -and-keep-it.

9. Meyer, *Setting the Table*, 235.

10. John F. Helliwell, Richard Layard, and Jeffrey Sachs, eds., 2015, *World Happiness Report 2015*. New York: Sustainable Development Solutions Network.

11. Adam Grant, "How to Succeed Professionally by Helping Others," *The Atlantic*, March 17, 2014, https://www.theatlantic.com/health /archive/2014/03/how-to-succeed-professionally-by-helping -others/284429/.

12. "On the Costs of Self-interested Economic Behavior," Philosophy of the Social Sciences. Accessed July 16, 2018, http://journals.sagepub .com/doi/abs/10.1177/1359105309356366.

13. "Virtue Rewarded: Helping Others at Work Makes People Happier," *University of Wisconsin News*, July 29, 2013, http://news.wisc.edu /virtue-rewarded-helping-others-at-work-makes-people-happier/.

14. Margot Andersen, "Why Great Leaders Are Generous Leaders," *The Career Diplomat*, October 31, 2016, http://thecareerdiplomat.com /why-great-leaders-are-generous-leaders/.

15. Adam Gopnik, *The Table Comes First* (New York: Vintage Books, 2011), 112.

16. Matthew Dixon, Nick Toman, and Rick DeLisi, *The Effortless Experience Conquering the New Battleground for Customer Loyalty* (New York: Portfolio/Penguin, 2013).

17. Helen Fisher, "We Have Chemistry!" helenfisher.com, n.d, http://www.helenfisher.com/downloads/articles/ArticleWe Have Chemistry.pdf. See also Alison Beard, "If You Understand How the Brain Works, You Can Reach Anyone: A Conversation With Biological Anthropologist Helen Fisher," *Harvard Business Review*, March–April 2017, 62.

18. Excerpted from "The secret to delighting customers: Putting employees first," March 2016, McKinsey & Company, www.mckinsey.com.

CHAPTER 9

1. Joseph Grenny, "You Might Be the Reason Your Employees Aren't Changing," HBR.org, February 17, 2015, https://hbr.org/2015/02 /you-might-be-the-reason-your-employees-arent-changing.

2. Rob Markey, "Earn Customer Loyalty Without Losing Your Shirt," *Harvard Business Review,* July 23, 2014. Accessed June 8, 2018, https://hbr.org/2012/07/earn-customer-loyalty-without.

3. Ibid.

CHAPTER 10

1. Fred Reichheld, "Car Rental Experience That Hurts," *Net Promoter Blog*, March 20, 2006, http://netpromoter.typepad.com/fred _reichheld/.

2. Joel Maynes & Alex Rawson, "Linking the Customer Experience to Value," McKinsey & Company Marketing & Sales, March 2016, http://www.mckinsey.com/business-functions/marketing-and-sales /our-insights/linking-the-customer-experience-to-value.

3. Hershey H. Friedman and Achmed Rahman, "Gifts Upon Entry and Appreciatory Comments: Reciprocity Effects in Retailing," *Journal of International Marketing Studies*, vol. 3, no. 3 (September 2011), 161.

4. Andy Tarnoff, "Customer Service Still Makes the Difference at Mequon Ace," OnMilwaukee.com, March 14, 2017, https: //onmilwaukee.com/market/articles/mequon-ace-hardware.html.

5.   Scott Gerber, "13 Ways to Surprise and Delight Your Customers Today," BPlans.com, n.d, http://articles.bplans.com/13-ways-to -surprise-and-delight-your-customers-today/.

CHAPTER 11

1.   Jeffrey N. Doucette, "What's Your Legacy?" *Nursing Management*, vol. 44, no. 9, September 2013, 6.

2.   Glenn Llopis, "5 Ways a Legacy-Driven Mindset Will Define Your Leadership," *Forbes*, February 20, 2014, https://www.forbes.com /sites/glennllopis/2014/02/20/5-ways-a-legacy-driven-mindset-will -define-your-leadership/#79e8b38116b1.

3.   David Brooks, "The Moral Bucket List," *New York Times*, April 11, 2015, https://www.nytimes.com/2015/04/12/opinion/sunday /david-brooks-the-moral-bucket-list.html?_r=0.

4.   In "The Role of Emotional Intelligence in Real Customer Engagement," Peoplemetrics.com, February 10, 2011, http://www .peoplemetrics.com/blog/the-role-of-emotional-intelligence-in -delivering-authentic-customer-service.

5.   Katrina Brooker, "The Chairman of the Board Looks Back," *Fortune*, May 28, 2001, http://archive.fortune.com/magazines/fortune /fortune_archive/2001/05/28/303852/index.htm.

6.   "Making Change (in Multiples)," *Seth's Blog*, February 13, 2017. Accessed June 8, 2018, https://seths.blog/2017/02/making-change -in-multiples/.

7.   Dave Ulrich, *The Leadership Capital Index: Realizing the Market Value of Leadership* (Oakland: Berrett-Koehler Publishers, Kindle Edition, 2015).

INDEX

ABOUT THE AUTHORS

SANDY ROGERS

Sandy Rogers founded and leads FranklinCovey's Loyalty Practice, a FranklinCovey offering that helps organizations increase customer and employee loyalty. He was previously Senior Vice President at Enterprise Rent-A-Car. During his fourteen years there, Sandy managed the turnaround of the London, England, operation and led the teams that developed Enterprise's marketing and fleet services strategies, the advertising campaign "Pick Enterprise . . . We'll Pick You Up," and the system for measuring and improving customer service across all branches. Before Enterprise, he worked in marketing at Apple Computer, and in brand management at P&G. Sandy has a bachelor's degree from Duke and an MBA from Harvard Business School.

LEENA RINNE

Leena Rinne is FranklinCovey's Vice President of Consulting. She is responsible for the hiring, development, and management of FranklinCovey's world-class consultant team and is responsible for the ongoing high-quality delivery of its programs and solutions. Leena spent six years as a FranklinCovey Senior Consultant, focused on individual effectiveness and leadership development. She worked with leaders from the C-suite to entry-level managers to diagnose organizational gaps and develop solutions that achieved lasting change and measurable results. Prior to consulting, Leena was FranklinCovey's International Business Partner Lead, overseeing the operational support for thirty-nine licensed partners globally. Leena was part of the Innovations team that developed several core content areas, including *The 7 Habits of Highly Effective People, Signature Edition 4.0*, and *The 5 Choices to Extraordinary Productivity*. She is co-author of the *Wall Street Journal* best-selling book *The 5 Choices: The Path to Extraordinary Productivity*.

SHAWN MOON

Shawn has over three decades of experience in leadership and management, sales and marketing, program development, and consulting services. He led FranklinCovey's Direct Offices, as well as the Execution, Speed of Trust, Customer Loyalty, and Sales Performance Practices. He is the author or co-author of several books, including *The Ultimate Competitive Advantage, Talent Unleashed*, and *Building a Winning Culture in Government*.

SCHEDULE AN AUTHOR
TO SPEAK AT YOUR EVENT

SANDY **ROGERS**   LEENA **RINNE**   SHAWN **MOON**

Are you planning an event for your organization? Schedule a *Leading Loyalty* author to deliver an engaging keynote speech tailor-made for today's leaders at events including:

- Association and Industry Conferences
- Sales Conferences
- Executive and Board Retreats

- Annual Meetings
- Company Functions
- Onsite Consulting
- Client Engagements

These authors have spoken at hundreds of conferences and client events worldwide.

To schedule one of the authors today, call
1-888-554-1776
or visit leadingloyaltybook.com.

FranklinCovey.

THE ULTIMATE COMPETITIVE ADVANTAGE

TAKE THE NEXT STEP IN YOUR JOURNEY

PARTICIPATE IN A TWO-DAY *ULTIMATE LOYALTY* WORK SESSION

Continue your journey toward leading loyalty by attending the work session *Ultimate Loyalty: Building Teams That Wow Customers*. Attend this two-day experience to learn the principles and practices needed to earn the loyalty of employees and customers. By implementing a series of strategic huddles, you will discover how to model, teach, and reinforce empathy, responsibility, and generosity.

In this two-day work session, you will learn to:
- Build employee loyalty first, then customer loyalty.
- Align the customer experience with customer expectations.
- Understand how to model, teach, and reinforce the behaviors to earn loyalty.
- Adopt a deliberate, consistent process toward customer service.
- Execute strategies to discover your customers' underlying goals.

To register or for more information, visit
FRANKLINCOVEY.COM/LOYALTYWORKSESSION
or call 1-888-868-1776.

FranklinCovey has partnered with American Management Association® to make this two-day work session available to you Live In-Person or Live Online.

FranklinCovey
ALL ACCESS PASS®

The FranklinCovey All Access Pass provides unlimited access to our best-in-class content and solutions, allowing you to expand your reach, achieve your business objectives, and sustainably impact performance across your organization.

AS A PASSHOLDER, YOU CAN:

- Access FranklinCovey's world-class content, whenever and wherever you need it, including *The 7 Habits of Highly Effective People®: Signature Edition 4.0*, *Leading at the Speed of Trust®*, and *The 5 Choices to Extraordinary Productivity®*.

- Certify your internal facilitators to teach our content, deploy FranklinCovey consultants, or use digital content to reach your learners with the behavior-changing content you require.

- Have access to a certified implementation specialist who will help design impact journeys for behavior change.

- Organize FranklinCovey content around your specific business-related needs.

- Build a common learning experience throughout your entire global organization with our core-content areas, localized into 16 languages.

Join thousands of organizations using the All Access Pass to implement strategy, close operational gaps, increase sales, drive customer loyalty, and improve employee engagement.

To learn more, visit
FRANKLINCOVEY.COM or call **1-888-868-1776**.

FranklinCovey
THE ULTIMATE COMPETITIVE ADVANTAGE